THE GUSTAVE A. AND MAMIE W.
EFROYMSON MEMORIAL LECTURES
DELIVERED AT THE
HEBREW UNION COLLEGE-JEWISH
INSTITUTE OF RELIGION
IN THE SPRING OF 1986

T0125155

THE GUSTAVE A. AND MAMIE W. EFROYMSON MEMORIAL LECTURES

Haim M. I. Gevaryahu
"The Theology and Biblical Scholarship of Yehezkel Kaufmann"

Arnaldo Momigliano
"Aspects of Judaism from the Hellenic and the Roman Angle"

Eliezer Schweid
"Jewish Survival in Exile: An Israeli View"

Bernard Lewis
"The Jews of Islam"

George L. Mosse
"German Jews Beyond Judaism"

David Winston
"Logos and Mystical Theology in Philo of Alexandria"

Arthur Green
"Devotion and Commandment: The Faith of Abraham in the Hasidic Imagination"

Peter Gay
"A Godless Jew: Freud, Atheism, and the Making of Psychoanalysis"

Louis Jacobs
"God, Torah, Israel: Traditionalism Without Fundamentalism"

Devotion and Commandment

*The Faith of Abraham
in the
Hasidic Imagination*

ARTHUR GREEN

HEBREW UNION COLLEGE PRESS
UNIVERSITY OF PITTSBURGH PRESS

© Copyright 1989 by the Hebrew Union College Press
Hebrew Union College-Jewish Institute of Religion

 "The Gustave A. and Mamie W. Efroymson memorial lectures delivered at the
Hebrew Union College-Jewish Institute of Religion in the spring of 1986"

ISBN 13: 978-0-8229-6394-3
ISBN 10: 0-8229-6394-9

Acknowledgments

I wish to take this opportunity to express my gratitude to the faculty of the Hebrew Union College-Jewish Institute of Religion for inviting me to deliver these lectures. Professor Jakob Petuchowski was the original bearer of the invitation, and Professor Michael Cook was my gracious host while in Cincinnati. I am grateful to both of them. Professor Michael Meyer has been a patient and long-suffering editor. As one whose scholarly work is now combined with full-time academic administration, I am thankful for his patience.

The preparation of these lectures in written form would not have been possible without the help of my student and research assistant Caryn Broitman and the able hand of my secretary Evelyn Gechman. My thanks to both of them.

The lectures that make up this volume emerged in response to an ongoing series of questions by students in courses on Hasidism taught over the past twenty years in three educational settings: Havurat Shalom community, the University of Pennsylvania, and the Reconstructionist Rabbinical College. I am happy to dedicate this study to my students, who throughout these years have been an endless source of intellectual stimulation and personal reward.

I

One of the most puzzling paradoxes in the history of religion is the complex and often ambivalent relationship that religious communities have had with those visionary leaders who stand at the pinnacle of the ongoing human striving for encounter with divinity. Would-be prophets and mystics, including those venerated by countless generations of later faithful, in their own day find themselves at odds with the religious community and its leadership. That which happened to Jesus and Mohammed happened also to countless others whom history has judged less kindly. The prophets of ancient Israel, whether regarded later as "true" or "false," had less than an easy time with the pious of their generations. Nor were their conflicts necessarily authority struggles in which the popular holy men were pitted against the ecclesiastical establishments of their times. Later disciples, to be sure, often like to depict the half-forgotten struggles of their masters in this way, trying to claim the faithful masses of "those times" as their own, while vilifying the leaders who were blind to their masters' truth. In reality, however, usually the masses along with their leaders rejected the "new" messages brought by seers fresh from direct encounters with the heavenly forces. Faithful and leaders alike are deeply invested in the mediating structures of religion, and these are ever threatened by the greater power of unmediated encounters with divinity.

Religion, after all, is about mediation. The *mysterium tremendum et fascinans* attracts and frightens at once. As much as we seek in religion a path to bring us closer to the great power of divinity, we look to it also to protect us from that same power. Priests, sacraments, commandments, holy times and sacred places, ceremonies, rites, and symbols all serve as relatively "safe" conductors for human contact with divinity. The function of ritual form in *zimzum ha-shefa'* (literally: "the contraction of the influx"), as it is called in Hebrew, is well understood by Jewish mystics through the ages, as by their compatriots in other traditions, as a necessary compromise religion must make with the frailty of human nature. That which to the priest is the very essence of the sacred may appear to the prophet or mystic in a more ambiguous light. The form indeed may be a bearer of true holiness; as such, however, it both enables us to see the divine that would remain invisible without it and blinds us by its own brightness to the divinity which also fills all that surrounds it.[1]

This encounter of the mystic or prophet with the mediating agencies of religion is one of those points of tension at which the two faces of the human religious enterprise most clearly reveal themselves: religion as the striving of the individual for inwardness, transcendence, or direct access to divinity, and religion as a group's articulation of its system of meaning, the "social construction of reality." The interaction between these two aspects of religion, as the "spiritual" or charismatic figure encounters them, always has a multifaceted character. The impatience with church, law, or doctrine, so typical of mysticism on one level, is matched, sometimes in the selfsame mystics, by an extreme devotion to those very forms or images within the tradition that would most seem to stand as barriers to the sort of immediate encounter with the One that characterizes the mystic's search. It is the training and inner growth within the framework offered by those very forms, after all, that has brought the mystic to the point of that encounter. This personal history almost inevitably creates in the mystic a loyalty to the forms with which he or she was nurtured.

For rabbinic Jews, mediation between God and His people Israel takes place through the revealed Torah and its commandments. In this Judaism's remarkable verbocentric recasting of biblical religion, God is depicted as One known almost exclusively through the articulation of His will as verbally transmitted through Moses' prophecy. It is the *word* of God alone that makes God manifest, the word as manifest in the commandments and narratives of Scripture, in the tales told by the Rabbis, and in the ongoing process of oral interpretation of the text. Access to God through such extra-verbal means as appreciation of His created handiwork is not denied by the Rabbis, but neither is it particularly encouraged; nor does it play a major role in rabbinic religion. Access via experiences of prophecy in post-biblical times is openly denied as a threat to the verbal canon.[2] Study of Torah and the daily fulfillment of its commandments, the twin chief virtues of rabbinic Judaism, are the ways one serves, pleases, and communes with the transcendent but ever-present God.

The relationship of the medieval Kabbalists to issues of authority and mediation has been discussed by Gershom Scholem in his landmark essay "Religious Authority and Mysticism" and elsewhere.[3] Scholem notes the essentially conservative character of early Kabbalah, a movement that arose in large measure as a part of the inner Jewish reaction against the universalist and spiritualizing tendencies of medieval Aristotelianism. Kabbalistic symbolism, deeply rooted in the imagery of biblical and rabbinic sources, served especially to provide a new layer of sacramental meaning to the *halakhah*. In fact, the literature of *ta'amey ha-mizvot*, the reasons for the commandments, was a major area of Kabbalistic creativity.[4] On the other hand, Scholem points to the mystical heresies of seventeenth- and eighteenth-century Judaism, centering around the messianic claim of Sabbatai Zevi, as Judaism's primary exemplification of mystical/ecstatic rejection of authority, a phenomenon which he does not fail to compare to the rejection of the Law in the chiliastic enthusiasm of early Christianity. It is also clear to one who follows the intricacies of Scholem's dialectical presentation that the roots of this seventeenth-century rebellion are to be found in the classical Kabbalah itself, beginning with the assumption, shared by philosophers and Kabbalists, that there is a hidden spiritual meaning which is of higher or deeper value than the rather worldly-seeming text of the written Torah. Claim as the orthodox Kabbalist might that the inner chambers of Torah and of the soul can be reached only through the outer, the very positing of such a distinction sets the stage for a radical transvaluation in which exoteric religion will eventually come to be seen as the enemy of true spirituality rather than as the only means of access to it.[5]

The case of Hasidism, a latter-day popular version of Jewish mystical teachings, is a particularly interesting one in which to examine the relationship of mystical religion and the agencies of mediation, and one which Scholem did not treat in this context. The early Hasidic masters, charismatic and revivalist mystics of the first order, were accused by their enemies in the rabbinic camp of heresy, of deviance from the norms of Jewish practice, and of dangerous promulgation among the unlettered of an esoteric doctrine that was best kept secret.[6] The *ḥasidim*, faithful in fact to practice in almost every area, took great pains to present themselves as a revival movement entirely within the pale of Jewish orthodoxy, not least in order to appease their fierce and powerful opponents. The movement also underwent a major shift in its place within the Eastern European Jewish community early in the course of its history. Hasidism started out in the position of an opposition movement vis-à-vis what it depicted as stultified and remote rabbinic leadership. As such it saw no reason to hesitate in advocating the ready accessibility of God's direct presence in a life of joyous piety that could be lived even by relatively unlearned and simple Jews who as a matter of course conducted themselves within the regimen of *halakhah*. Perceiving no threat to the norms of praxis *per se*, its leaders spoke freely of a divinity present in all human thoughts and deeds, not only in the ritual forms specifically associated with institutional religion.[7] The first Hasidic masters saw themselves in the role of gadfly to the religious establishment, denouncing sham, mere outward attention to detail, and a tradition of learning that had become elitist and detached from the religious needs of the broader community. By the second decade of the nineteenth century, however, some fifty years into the movement's history, Hasidism's success had made *it* the establishment. The rabbinic opposition had become quiescent, and a new enemy, indeed a threat to the halakhic order, was seen in the *haskalah* movement that had begun to take root in Austrian Galicia and even, to a lesser degree, across the Russian border. Now Hasidism felt a need to take up the defense of tradition as its most urgent agenda,[8] a role that increased with the decline of religious observance throughout the nineteenth century, leading Hasidism into the position of ultra-orthodoxy with which it is identified in recent times.

In order to see the tension between mysticism and mediation in Hasidism, therefore, we must limit ourselves mostly to the early decades of the movement's literary creativity.[9] We must also take care not to see the early masters through the eyes of later disciples who have refashioned them in their own image. To see Hasidism as a movement of radical spiritual revival in tension with the mediating forces of religion we must especially turn our attention to the circle around Dov Baer of Miedzyrzec (d. 1772), the first great organizer of the Hasidic movement. Since the writings of Dov Baer and a number of his immediate disciples are preserved in editions that were already in print around the turn of the nineteenth century, we are in a remarkably good position to examine a group of primary sources written (or at least preached) in the early and heady days of Hasidic revival.[10]

Dov Baer, or the Maggid ("preacher"), as he is called, was the one who put the simple revivalist insights of his teacher, Israel Ba'al Shem Tov (1700–1760), the first central figure of Hasidism, into the framework of a full-blown mystical theology. The language he used was that of the earlier Kabbalah, but the meaning of the words was shifted drastically and the mythic cosmology which lay at the heart of Kabbalism was largely vitiated. What remained was a theology that bordered on acosmicism, in which God was the only reality and all else, including individual human identity, was but a veil of illusion.[11] Versions of the Maggid's teaching as preserved by his various disciples differ in the degree to which he insisted on the illusory quality of worldly existence, but the general thrust of his teaching is clear. Some renditions of early Hasidic mysticism are indeed more world-affirming, but only in the sense that all objects, places, and moments may become openings in which to discover the all-pervasive presence of God, or to see that all reality is a "garbing" of the single divine life-flow.[12] This sense of the ultimate unreality of all existence other than that of God was accompanied by a mystical psychology directed toward the cultivation of those states of mind that might lead the devotee toward an experiential realization of that acosmic truth.

A certain degree of anti-intellectualism, though sometimes exaggerated in modern accounts of Hasidism, was also present in the movement. The preachers' circles in which Hasidism was first articulated were opposed, as we have noted, to the abstruse learning of the rabbinic elite, often depicted by its critics as a learning used more to display academic virtuosity than to clarify God's law, its ostensible chief subject matter. While *hasidim* shared in the general Eastern European Jewish commitment to talmudic learning, the early sources express some hesitation about whether such study truly brings one to attachment to God. Constant exertion of the mind in the gymnastics of *pilpul* seems not to leave room for the infinitely simpler insight that "the whole earth is full of His glory," an insight which itself needs full attention of mind in order to be truly realized.[13] While there were talmudic scholars of note among the leaders of Hasidism in later generations, it seems fair to say that in the early years most recognized scholars opposed the movement. In early Hasidism the mediating act of Torah study was in fact reconceptualized. Study remained important, but it was the sort of study that itself led to a much more immediate contact with divinity. Hasidic study would involve the Torah text itself, certain well-worn passages of talmudic *aggadah*, and a few works of earlier Jewish mystics and moralists.[14] The much more difficult and less directly rewarding (from the spiritualist point of view) large legal tractates of the Talmud and their earlier and later commentators were mostly set aside. Torah was read from a quasi-pneumatic point of view: a homily had to weave together insights from a pastiche of verses and passages, as had always been true; but it also had to cast light on how this passage of the Torah shows that God is present to His people at all times, in all places—even in this very moment.

> He who wants to interpret the Torah has to begin by drawing unto himself words as hot as burning coals. Speech comes out of the upper heart, which Scripture calls "the rock of my heart" (Ps. 73:26). The interpreter [first] has to pour out his words to God in prayer, seeking to arouse His mercies, so that this heart will open. Speech then flows from the heart, and the interpretation of Torah comes from that speech. . . . As the Heart's compassion is opened, it gives forth blazing

words, as it is written: "My heart blazes within me; the fire of my words burns on my tongue." (Ps. 39:3).[15]

Another master speaks of preaching words of Torah as a form of automatic speech, in which the conscious mind is quiescent and the teacher becomes but a mouthpiece for the self-articulating divine word.[16] The change in Torah study was characterized by a rereading of the Talmud's own characterization of true study, *Torah li-shemah* (lit.: "for" or "in her name"). The Hasidic authors insist that this rubric does not justify "study for *its own* sake" but rather "study for *her* sake," for the sake of the *shekhinah*, the indwelling presence of God.[17] Such "study," unlike the ordinary give-and-take of talmudic discourse, would involve direct discussion of "matters of the spirit," even when not reaching the pneumatic heights described above.

Here we see the mystic in struggle with mediation. His own sense of direct encounter with divinity has made it clear to him that the intellectualized religion of the Rabbis is inadequate. Rather than fight the central Jewish institution of *talmud torah*, however, he has converted it to his own purposes. The prime value of the Eastern European rabbinate has been significantly transformed. Study has been so redefined as to make it an adjunct to preaching, itself a means of spiritual arousal.

On the question of study, Hasidic mysticism was in this way able to achieve a certain truce with the rabbinic tradition.[18] On the twin issue of the commandments and their role in the religious life, however, the conflicts with the movement's mystical revivalist values cut much deeper. In such a religious worldview, the place of law and religious praxis would almost of necessity have to be questioned. If corporeal existence itself is illusory and the purpose of the religious quest is to see beyond its veil, why should God demand of us the very sort of actions that seem to bind us to the material world? *Halakhah* leads us to constant concern with minutiae of time and space, with details of such worldly matters as the *kashrut* of cooking pots, the precise hour when prayers are to be recited, the proper preparation of ritual objects, examination for states of ritual impurity, and the like. How can the one who seeks only God be bothered with such matters? Can *devequt*, the state of utter attachment to God, or *biṭṭul*, the mystical negation of the ego-self, be achieved by such seemingly worldly and small-minded concerns? On the other hand, to the extent that this world does have a degree of reality and can itself be a way of finding God, is His divinity not equally spread throughout all Creation? Isaiah's "the whole earth is filled with His glory" becomes an ecstatic watchword in a Hasidism that proclaims "God needs to be served in all ways,"[19] in all of human life. What room remains then for Judaism's rigid separation between the holy and the profane, between that permitted by sacred law and that forbidden? There is a seeming pettiness of concern within the halakhic mindset that offends the devotional ideal of "expanding the borders of the holy." In short, the phenomenal world is either entirely illusory or entirely holy, at least in potential. The intermediate position, clearly that of rabbinic religion, seems hardest to defend in the world of radical spiritualist thinking.

The disciples of the Maggid knew full well that they were not about to set aside the halakhic system in practice. It may indeed have been this very knowledge and the security it offered that allowed them the inner freedom to play out their radicalism in the realm of spirit. While there is a good deal of variety within the school, such prominent members of the circle as Levi Yizhak of Berdichev (c. 1740–1810) and Menahem Mendel of Vitebsk (1730–1788) record in their homilies traces of significant inner turmoil on the question of the place of law and commandments in the face of the single all-embracing commandment to strive without compromise for intimate union with God. In a text I have translated elsewhere,[20] Levi Yizhak puts the argument against the commandments in the mouth of the snake in Eden. Eve was tempted by an argument that ran something like this: "How can the God who affirms the goodness of all of His creation have created a tree whose fruit would cause harm? Surely the implied affirmation of the Creation ('God saw that it was good') should take precedence over the seemingly arbitrary prohibition of the Tree of Knowledge." Elsewhere it is to the messianic future rather than to the Edenic past that the mystic turns, expressing a confidence, rooted in rabbinic tradition itself, that the commandments will one day pass away, leaving the mystic the possibility of serving God with the purity of spiritual worship alone.

II

Our concern for much of this study will be with one series of discussions of this topic, those centering around the patriarchs, particularly Abraham, and the nature of their religious lives. A large number of Hasidic sources use Abraham and his religious life as a relatively "safe" way of discussing the tension they feel around the issue of commandment and spirit. While it is seemingly clear in the biblical narrative that the patriarchs, living before Sinai, had no relationship to the Torah and its commandments, the early Rabbis insist, quite to the contrary, that Torah in all its details was both observed and studied in patriarchal times. This claim is unequivocally stated in the well-known talmudic dictum that "Abraham our Father fulfilled the entire Torah before it was given, even '*eruv tavshilin*" (the purely rabbinic device for permitting the preparation of Sabbath food on the preceding festival day).[21] While this seemingly surprising assertion fits the general pattern of the Rabbis' conversion of all the biblical heroes into practicing rabbinic Jews, it also has the specific force of claiming that from the very outset there is no Judaism without the Law. I will argue below that the need for such an assertion grew out of the early Jewish-Christian polemic, especially out of the Pauline use of Abraham as the exemplar of one who served God in "faith" or "spirit" before the Law was given.

The rabbinic sources on Abraham were of course known to the Hasidic masters as a part of the vast halakhic and aggadic edifice which claimed the loyalty of every pious Jew. They were, in Hasidism as earlier, the object of both veneration and commentary. While belief in the truth of Scripture was seen as binding, as was acceptance of the authority of *halakhah*, the relationship of later

Jews to the non-legal portions of the rabbinic corpus (*aggadah*) was more complicated. A rare figure of the courage and stature of a Maimonides could dare to state openly the impossibility of an intelligent person committing himself to a literal belief in the Rabbis' tales and interpretations.[22] He gave open expression to a widely held belief which insisted that the words of the sages must *somehow* be true, but in a non-literal sense. Many generations of homilists and commentators sought valiantly—sometimes almost desperately—to defend the *aggadah* by seeking deeper meaning behind it.[23] When dealing with such an aggadic statement as the claim that Abraham kept the commandments, the Hasidic authors probably believed in its literal truth (partly, to be sure, because no one could picture him violating them). At the same time, this tradition, like all others, both biblical and rabbinic, could be the occasion for new homiletical comment.

We turn now to an examination of several Hasidic preachers and the ways in which they are seen both making use of and struggling with this inherited rabbinic/Kabbalistic tradition. Our interest will be in seeing how the claim that Abraham observed the commandments is *spiritualized* in Hasidism by a homiletic attempt to read into the patriarch not the rabbinic insistence on literal conformity with the Torah but rather the Hasidic message of attachment to God through the negation of the corporeal self. Hopefully it will become clear, in the course of our reading, that the Hasidic theologians, not unlike the first great theologian of Christianity, are using the figure of Abraham as a locus for discussing their own struggles with the nature of Torah observance and its place within the life of religious devotion.

We begin with a relatively "conservative" passage by Levi Yizhak of Berdichev, in which the talmudic claim receives a typically Hasidic explanation:

> Our sages said that Abraham fulfilled the entire Torah, even *'eruv tavshilin*, before it was given. But how did Abraham, peace be upon him, know the Torah before it was given? We know, however, that the 248 positive commandments [of the Torah] parallel the 248 spiritual limbs and the 365 prohibitions parallel the 365 spiritual sinews. One who looks into the spirituality of his own limbs and

sinews grasps the 248 positive and 365 negative commandments. Just as the bodily limbs require certain material food and other aids for sustenance, each limb having its own needs, so does each of the spiritual limbs require its own *mizvah*. As the limbs of the physical body do not need to be taught what it is that they require, so too the limbs of the spirit: they attain to the commandments of their own accord. In fact the very life-essence of the spiritual limbs themselves is the positive commandments, and the life-essence of the sinews is the negative commandments. Spirituality is the most subtle form of intellect or thought, and the purest level of thought is nought but the commandments. Thus he who achieves transcendence of the corporeal, as was the case at Sinai, is attached to the light of his intellect in positive and negative commandments, for the light of intellect is nothing but the fulfillment of positive commandments and the observance of prohibitions. . . . Thus it was possible, before the Torah was given, to fulfill all the commandments. The reason we do not grasp the Torah from within our own minds is that corporeality drops a curtain that separates us from attainment of the spiritual light. . . . Abraham our Father, peace be upon him, whose corporeal self was purified, grasped from his own 248 limbs and 365 sinews the spirituality of the entire Torah before it was given.[24]

The author introduces us here to a world of traditional Jewish mythology, some understanding of which is required in order for us to appreciate his comment. The number of the Torah's commandments has been fixed at 613 since Amoraic times (third century). According to a well-known talmudic passage, these are divided between 248 positive commandments, corresponding to the limbs of the body, and 365 prohibitions, corresponding to the days of the solar year.[25] The point seems to be that the entire self must be constantly involved in the life of the commandments. Later Jewish speculations[26] associated the number 365 with the "sinews" rather than with the calendar out of a belief that the Torah and the human being reflected the same inner structure. According to such a theory, the fulfillment of the commandments is nothing other than the true fulfillment of the self. The idea of creation in the divine image is thus overlaid by the medieval Kabbalist with a typically formulaic superstructure.

Levi Yizhak, who was something of a realist as a spiritual teacher, has to confront a problem in this received tradition. How is it that this correspondence between self and Torah is not obvious to us? Why do we not feel or hear each limb calling out for the fulfillment of a *mizvah*?[27] His answer is a classic bit of preacher's moralizing: indeed the inner limbs and sinews do call out to us, each one reaching for the fulfillment of its own *mizvah*. The problem is that we materialistic beings are so preoccupied with satisfying the corporeal self that we give no heed to the spiritual outcry from within. Only such a saintly figure as Abraham, who had overcome his own material nature, could give full attention to the sustenance of the spiritual self by means of the commandments.

In the course of this discussion, Levi Yizhak mentions yet another idea that requires some clarification. "Spirituality," he says, "is the most subtle form of intellect or thought, and the purest level of thought is nought but the commandments." The spiritual quest, says the Hasidic master, is a journey inward to the most subtle reaches of the mind. This voyage within the self corresponds to an "upward" journey on the cosmic map of the *sefirot*, the inner gradations of divinity, that stand as the foundation upon which the entire edifice of Kabbalistic thought is elaborated. A journey to the "most subtle form of intellect" is the inward move to *hokhmah*, the primal point of intellect on the sefirotic map. But *hokhmah* is also the place of Torah's origin, or the point on the map where the hidden will of God (*keter*) begins to make itself manifest in the form of primal text. *Keter*, as the will of God, is the source of the commandments, and thus stands at the far reach of the mind's innermost depths. This correspondence deepens the network of association between the journey inward, exemplified here by Abraham's discovery of truth from within, and the religion of the *mizvot*. The journey to God via the inner self and the journey to God along the path of the commandments are of necessity the selfsame journey. To cast his text in light of our previous discussion, we might say that here Torah has been utilized in a particularly mystical reading of the mediative role: Torah *is* the identical inner structure of self and divinity that allows our immediate experience of God to take place.

But, according to this passage, did Abraham actually, that is, in a material sense, observe all the commandments? A careful reading shows a certain amount of equivocation. He attained "the spirituality of the entire Torah" before it was given, a spirituality that in fact inhabits the deep structures of the human mind itself, according to Levi Yizhak. But did this attainment actually convert itself into observance on the physical plane? Here our author remains somehow silent. We shall return later to Levi Yizhak for what may be a clarification of his position, but first we turn elsewhere for a more unqualified view of Abraham's wholly spiritual fulfillment of the Law.

Hasidic statements on Abraham and the *mizvot* generally appear in the literature in a homiletical context, in the way most Hasidic teachings are preserved. They occur most frequently in comments on Genesis 26:5: "Because Abraham listened to My voice and kept My guard, My commandments, statutes, and teachings"— the same verse on which the Talmud bases its claim. In reading these comments, however, it is important to recall that the Hasidic masters were preachers rather than biblical exegetes. In fact, the Hasidic teachings we have are made up almost entirely of condensed Hebrew translations of lengthy sermons preached in Yiddish.[28] The preacher, unlike the commentator, is motivated primarily by contemporary issues rather than by a problem in the text before him. In the case of Hasidic sermons, these are often devotional issues. Thus the statements on Abraham and the commandments usually appear in some relationship to a discussion of "true" worship in our own times as well, serving as paradigm, as contrast, or sometimes as both. In the following passage, which appears in a homily for Sukkot, Kalonymos Kalman Epstein of Cracow (d. 1823) is discussing the *sukkah* and its structure as a paradigm for the devotional life. In the course of this discussion he says:

> The *zaddiq*, one who has already attained the state of attachment to the Endless One and remains bound there constantly in his thought, worships primarily through contemplation. Thus [the Rabbis] said: "Abraham our Father fulfilled the entire Torah before it was given." Even though we find nowhere that he actually performed such commandments as donning *tefillin*, building a *sukkah*, or the like, he drew unto himself the inward holiness to which all of these deeds

point. He did this by his holy thought, which was attached to the
Endless One.[29]

Here our author speaks as something of a "realist" within the
mystical universe. Epstein surely realizes, even without the historical self-consciousness of moderns, that the notion of Abraham's
observing Sukkot is something of an absurdity. Jews dwell in
booths for a week during the fall harvest season "for I caused the
children of Israel to dwell in booths as I took them out of the Land
of Egypt" (Lev. 23:43). How, then, could Abraham be fulfilling
this *mizvah* some four hundred years earlier? The problem is resolved by a reference to a spiritual essence that underlies each of
the commandments. Abraham became attached to the "inward
holiness" to which each of the commandments refers; it was this
the Talmud meant in saying that he observed all the Law.

The idea that each of the *mizvot* corresponds to a particular
degree or realm of "inward holiness," expressed only haltingly
here, is stated more clearly in other Hasidic sermons.[30] Here we
see the Hasidic authors reflecting, in however popularized and
psychologized a manner, the central religious direction of Kabbalah, particularly in its later Lurianic form. This will require
some explanation. The thirteenth-century Kabbalists, we recall,
were conservatives as well as radical innovators. Their elaborate
and unique symbol system consisted almost wholly of traditional
elements, and it functioned most essentially to give deeper meaning
and thus reinforcement to observance of the commandments as
defined by the Rabbis.[31] The Kabbalah insisted that fulfillment
of the Torah had cosmic ramifications, that the union of the sefirotic world, and hence the flow of life-sustaining divine energy
into the universe, was dependent on Israel and on the *mizvot*.[32] In
discussing the details of how this unification of the divine worked
through the commandments, however, even the ingenuity of the
Zohar and its contemporaries found itself limited chiefly to a few
"secrets" which were repeated over and over again as each particular commandment was discussed. By far the greatest part of
these "secrets of the commandments" was devoted to the unification of the male and female principles within divinity, *tif'eret* and

malkhut. Others united the female with the agent of masculine power, *yesod.* Some referred to the union of right and left within the Godhead, *ḥesed* and *gevurah.* The motif of uniting the four central *sefirot* (*tif'eret/malkhut* and *ḥesed/gevurah*) was especially popular: such foursomes as the species of Sukkot or the Scripture sections of *tefillin* could be counted on to symbolize this four-fold union.

It was only the rewriting of Kabbalah by Isaac Luria's disciples in the late sixteenth century which created the full range of specifications upon which our Hasidic sources are dependent. The shattered divine universe, according to the Lurianists, is in the ongoing process of restoration. This *tiqqun* has to take place at every one of the rungs that collectively comprise the cosmos. The *sefirot,* here reconstituted as five *parzufim,*[33] each of which contains all others, are also said to exist in each of four "worlds." The new Kabbalistic symbol system thus starts out with a "grid" of one hundred elements (5x5x4) as opposed to the ten of the Zohar tradition.[34] The relationships among these elements are governed, *inter alia,* by the energy generated by performance of the commandments, each *mizvah* energizing a particular link in the ever-building chain of *tiqqun.* The cosmos-building energy contained within the *mizvah* is not, however, unlocked by the physical performance of the act alone. It is only the *mizvah* as performed by a self-conscious Kabbalist, aware of the power borne by the particular deed, that can have this effect. It may thus be said that it is the Kabbalist's concentration or devotional focus, combined with the prescribed act itself, that energizes the cosmos.

Here the Hasidic author is positing an important departure. Abraham, he suggests, was able to have the *kavvanah* or inward devotion associated with *tefillin* or *sukkah* without actually performing the commandment, and, in his age at least, the *kavvanah* alone was effective. In the case of those who lived before Sinai, one might legitimately conclude, it was devotional focus rather than commanded deed that worked to "repair" the cosmos. This possibility of separating *kavvanah* from deed, so obvious to moderns, was a radical innovation in Hasidic thought, even if confined to the ancient patriarchs. The inseparability of act and thought lay at the very heart of Kabbalah; it was their insistence on this union that allowed the Kabbalists to function as defenders of tradition. Now from within the pietistic camp we hear a voice that sounds just a bit like that of the medieval Aristotelian allegorizers, who were accused by their detractors of allowing profound thoughts to take the place of actual fulfillment of *mizvot*.[35]

Kalonymos Kalman Epstein was a disciple of Rabbi Elimelech of Lezajsk (1717–1787), author of the well-known homiletic collection *No'am Elimelech*. In that work, which, aside from its treatment of the *zaddiq* and his powers, has a markedly conservative theological character, there are two treatments of Abraham and the commandments. These claim that either by the path of self-purification and attachment to God (Elimelech was known for his devotion to ascetic practices) or by service through love, Abraham was able to reach into the "root" of each of the commandments. The term *shoresh* here seems to be used in a combination of the Kabbalistic sense that each *mizvah* has some particular root in the upper worlds and the Maimonidean sense of intellectual "roots" of the specific commandments. In Elimelech's discussions, as in many of the Hasidic treatments of this theme, the question of whether Abraham literally fulfilled the *mizvot* is left unanswered.[36]

This same notion of "getting to the root" of the commandments is used by a fellow member of the Miedzyrzec school, but in a much more radical way. Menahem Mendel of Vitebsk was one of the senior disciples of the Maggid. He became the first leader of Hasidism in Byelorussia, but in 1777 led a group of Beshtian *hasidim* to settle in *Erez Yisrael* and founded the Hasidic community of Tiberias. His teachings, collected in *Peri ha-Arez* and *Liqqutey 'Amarim*, are often among the more daring and revealing of early Hasidic documents. His comment on Abraham and the commandments comes in the midst of a discussion of Hillel's famous retort on the essence of Judaism to the prospective convert.[37] The negative form in which Hillel formulates his principle, "That which is hateful to you do not to your fellow," is due to the low rung on which the questioner is presumed to stand. It masks the true root of the commandments, "I am the Lord your God," which Hillel believes the convert is not yet ready to hear. But in the course of this discussion Menahem Mendel reveals a fascinating sense of hierarchy in the mystic's apprehension of the commandments:

All the roots and branches, general principles and specific rulings, having their root above, have borne fruit below in the performance of the commandments. This is our holy Torah, with all its commandments, statutes, and teachings. Our sages said on "Because Abraham listened to My voice and kept My guard" that Abraham kept the entire Torah, even *'eruvey tavshilin*. This surely seems strange; how did he know it? Even if we say that he apprehended those commandments that good sense would indicate, what about the statutes [*huqqim*], the red heifer and all the rest?[38] But . . . the sages tell us that God said to Moses, "To you I shall reveal the meaning of this heifer, but for others it will be a statute." The statutes too in fact have a meaning and a root above in the order of Creation, since Creation itself took place by means of Torah, but not every mind can bear this, and that is why "for others it will be a statute."[39] The Torah was not speaking of such giants as Moses or Abraham our Father, peace be upon them, before whom nothing stood as a statute. All the statutes were [comprehensible] commandments to them, as they apprehended their meaning and root. This transformation of statutes into commandments can only happen in a person for whom the [ordinary] commandments are negated, one to whom they do not apply. Such prohibitions as, for example, "Thou shalt not commit murder," "Thou shalt not commit adultery," and "Thou shalt not steal" are not appropriate to one who has broken down his desires, who makes use of his physical qualities never for himself but only for the sake of God. The fulfillment of his own needs is as repulsive to him as the filth of mud or excrement, from which any person, even without explicit warning, would naturally keep his distance. . . . A person like this, to whom the [other] commandments no longer apply, has revealed to him the reasons for the statutes, and they become to him as commandments. It is in this sense that our sages foretold that the commandments would be negated in messianic times,[40] for "earth will be filled with knowledge of the Lord" (Isa. 11:9). They will have another Torah, made up of statutes that have become commandments. But as one goes from strength to strength, proceeding ever upward, one reaches the root of the entire Torah and all the commandments, which is "I am the Lord your God," and boundless. As one stands there the power of all the commandments and statutes diminishes [lit.: "the wings are weakened"] and all of them are negated, since the evil urge itself has

been negated as one stands in that upper place which exists prior
to Creation.[41]

A passage like this makes it clear that in discussing the nature of
the *mizvot* in pre-Sinaitic times we are not dealing with idle speculations. Abraham's observance of the commandments is tied to
that which is to come in messianic times, but also what seems to
be, in a final burst that the author cannot control, that which
happens in the life of the *zaddiq* even now. The one who reaches
that eternal place of God's presence, *which is now as it was before
Creation*, is no longer subject to sin, therefore no longer liable to
commandment. All the specifications can thus return to their
source, and there stands but the simple commandment, the root
of all the others, "I am the Lord your God." The behavioral forms
associated with the religious life, both ritual and moral, are so
fully integrated in the life of the *zaddiq* that they no longer need
to be the subject of command.

Other passages claim that it was indeed through deeds, but
deeds other than those we perform since the giving of the Torah,
that the patriarchs fulfilled the commandments. While the commandments as such had not yet been given, the details of the
patriarchs' lives, as recorded in the Torah, are the bearers of this
kavvanah. Favorite candidates for such acts are the more inexpli-
cable and mystery-laden activities of the patriarchal narratives,
including Abraham and Isaac's digging of wells and Jacob's
seemingly unfathomable actions with the sticks in the breeding
of Laban's flock. The point of these accounts seems to be that
inwardness requires concretization in the ritual deed.[42] If those
acts which we perform, on the Torah's command, are not attested to in patriarchal times, there must have been others. Here the
Hasidic author is also able to explain why the holy Torah should
bother itself to tell us seemingly mundane details of our ancestors'
lives. One is tempted to see in these passages a certain admission
as to the arbitrariness of ritual activity (a sense that *any* act might
be the bearer of such *kavvanah*), but I would proceed with caution
in attributing such an awareness to the Hasidic writers. True,
these same figures claimed that God is to be served by all of

human actions and that "worship through corporeal things," that is, outside the commandments, was of great importance. At the same time, however, Hasidism did not fully separate itself from the theurgic sense that precise fulfillment of the specific *mizvot* had a cosmic effect, and the mysterious deeds of the patriarchs must be viewed in this light as well.[43]

Another version of this idea (one that the psychologist might find particularly interesting) claims that Abraham our Father observed all 613 commandments through the one commandment that he was in fact given according to the Torah text itself: that of circumcision. Noting that the word *berit*, or covenant of circumcision, is numerically equivalent to 613 (if we add one for the word itself), Rabbi Moses Hayim Ephraim of Sudilkow (c. 1740–1800), the grandson of the Ba'al Shem Tov, explains that

> all the commandments were included within it, so that from this single commandment Abraham looked upon all 613 commandments of the entire Torah and fulfilled each of the commandments through this one of the holy covenant that contains them all.

Referring to the parallel between the commandments and the limbs of the body, he goes on to say that

> in their day the Torah had not yet spread forth [into all the limbs], but was in a lesser state, concentrated in this single small limb which is the sign of the covenant.[44]

That is why, says the preacher of Sudilkow, the patriarchs sought to make converts: circumcision, including that of *gerim*, was the single act open to them through which the entire Torah could be fulfilled.

The final Hasidic text we shall consider in this series takes us back to Levi Yizhak of Berdichev. In a most surprising homily on the encounter of Abraham and Melchizedek, who is called by the Torah "a priest of the most high God" (Gen. 14:18), Levi Yizhak compares two sorts of divine service, that of the commandments, or Judaism as we know it, and the service of God through devotion (*mesirut nefesh*)[45] alone. While the homily is preserved in somewhat garbled form, as is often the case in the written sources of Hasidism, careful attention to it proves most rewarding for our search. Levi Yizhak claims that from the purely spiritualist viewpoint, including the accessibility of direct experience of God, service through devotion alone is in fact superior to that of the commandments. It is only the power of the *mizvot*, with their worldly focus, to bring blessing into the material universe, that ultimately makes them the proper focus of the Jew's religious life.

> "Melchizedek king of Shalem brought forth bread and wine; he was a priest of the most high God" (Gen. 14:18). The point is that there are two [types of] servants of God. One serves God by absolute devotion [*mesirut nefesh*] and the other by means of *mizvot* and good deeds. There is a difference between them; the one who serves God by devotion, without recourse to *mizvot* or good deeds, is in the Nought indeed,[46] while the one who serves through the commandments is worshiping by means of an existing thing. . . . Thus the one who serves through devotion cannot draw divine blessing upon himself, for he is nothing, being so attached to God. The one who serves by means of commandments and good deeds, attached to an existent, can bring divine blessing upon himself. . . .

We pause here in our reading to note that in this juxtaposition of two types, so typical of Hasidic sermons, the sympathies of the hearer should immediately fall to that side which worships by devotion alone. Being "in the Nought" is a clearly articulated goal of Hasidic mysticism, and attachment "to an existing thing" is an impediment to realizing this value. The attainment of *ayin* is the ultimate value in the teachings of Levi Yizhak's master, Dov Baer of Miedzyrzec, and several of his disciples. We wonder then whether there is not an inner Hasidic "address" for this homily. We also see here an interesting example of the inadequacy of traditional Hebrew terminology for expressing the real mystical content of the Hasidic message. The phrase "for he is nothing, being so attached to God," should really read "for he is nothing, being so 'absorbed' or 'consumed' in God," but the lexicon provided by earlier Kabbalistic usage did not provide anything stronger here than *dabbeq*. We now continue with a later portion of this text:

Our sages say that Abraham our Father fulfilled the entire Torah before it was given, even *'eruvey tavshilin*. We have tried to understand how he came to know the entire Torah. Because Abraham separated himself from the corporeal and saw that the life-force sustaining each of his own 248 limbs was from a particular *mizvah* and that without that *mizvah* the limbs would have no life, seeing, for example, that the life of the head was derived from *tefillin*, and so forth, he attained it all before it was given. . . . For this reason Abraham was not able to worship God outside the Land by means of the commandments. Outside the Land it was impossible to fulfill those commandments that apply only in the Land of Israel. Because the *mizvot* that correspond to certain limbs could not have been fulfilled, he would have been lacking those limbs. . . .[47] Thus it was that so long as Abraham dwelt outside the Land he served God through devotion. But when he entered the Land he was able to serve by means of the commandments in such a way as to be a complete form, with all his limbs, and he began to worship in that way. . . . Outside the Land, serving through devotion and 'attached' to the Nought, he was unable to bring the bounty of divine blessing upon himself. . . . Thus RaSHI comments on the verse "Get you forth from your land" (Gen. 12:1): "for your own benefit; for your own good". . . for you will be able to draw blessing upon yourself.

The original way of service given to or discovered by Abraham was in fact that of devotion, not that of *mizvot*. The reason Levi Yizhak gives for this is a surprising one. Abraham discovered God while yet living outside the Land of Israel. Had he tried to fulfill the commandments there, the network of correspondences between commandments and inner limbs would have left him lacking: such *mizvot* as tithes, sabbatical year, jubilee, and the entire sacrificial system are observable only in the Holy Land. As such his spiritual life would have been "deformed." Only on entering the Land of Israel was Abraham able to change his form of worship. It was for this reason, we presume, that the patriarch had no progeny until he came into the Land. Levi Yizhak goes on to discuss the differing levels of mystical vision reached by the two types of servants, again seeming to prefer the one who serves by devotion alone:

Now the one who serves God by devotion alone sees his blessed Creator with his very eyes, but the one who worships by means of *mizvot* and good deeds sees him through a glass [*aspeqlaryah*], since he is serving God through an existing thing.[48] This is the meaning of "After these things, God's word came to Abraham *in a vision*" (Gen. 15:1). Now he saw God through a glass. But the Lord said to him: "Fear not" because you are serving Me through commandments rather than through devotion. "Your reward is very great"—your service will be capable of bringing about blessing. . . . Thus Abraham's fulfillment of the Torah was only in the Land, but not outside it. But in our case, even though we are outside the Land, we are able to serve by means of *mizvot*, for [the Torah] has already been given.[49]

As Abraham comes into the Land he is possessed by fear. His relationship to God has changed; now that he worships through the commandments he no longer sees God "with his very eye" as he had previously. In other words, the level of direct religious experience accessible to Abraham has diminished as he has accepted the "yoke" of mediated religion. God Himself has to convince His faithful servant that such religion has in fact its own rewards. It may not lead to the same heights of inner vision, but it allows best for the presence of divine blessing in things of this world. (How clearly we see the Hasidic mystic reassuring himself!)

Only at the very end of Levi Yizhak's homily do we get back to Melchizedek, and then in a somewhat garbled way. He quotes a rabbinic discussion[50] of this passage, in which one speaker claims that the King of Shalem revealed to Abraham "the secret of the high priesthood," while the other claims it was "the secret of Torah" that Melchizedek revealed. "High priesthood," claims Levi Yizhak, refers to service through devotion, while "Torah" refers to the service by means of the *mizvot*. Clearly there is something missing in our record of this homily, and it is difficult to reconstruct just how it was that Melchizedek fit into this antinomy between devotion and commandment, an antinomy which Levi Yizhak qualifies further in the course of his discussion, claiming that *mizvot* really do have in them a degree of devotion as well. It seems highly unlikely, though not entirely inconceivable, that he was aware of the use made of this figure by Christian Scripture and imagination, in which Melchizedek is the paradigm of gentile priesthood and an antitype of Christ. Surely the characterization of Christianity as service through devotion and Judaism as service through Torah and deeds comes rather close to the stereotyping offered by Christians throughout the ages of the difference between the two traditions. It is hard to imagine the Hasidic author, innocent as he may have been of long-held polemical positions, accepting this typology and offering in Judaism's defense only the theurgic claim that service through the commandments was more efficacious in bringing divine bounty to the worshipper, especially in an age when Jews, to say the least, showed no evidence of having a monopoly on good fortune in the material world. But leaving the question of Christianity aside, the text remains a startling one. Abraham served God in a "higher" fashion before he came into the Land and began observing the commandments. He feared this lessening of his devotional intensity and had to be reassured by God. The point of this text is rather clear. Levi Yizhak recognizes that there is a way of worship that is "higher" in terms of the Hasidic values of radical spirituality than that of rabbinic Judaism. By service through pure devotion we could see God "with our very eye." But that level of mystical experience must be forsworn by the Jew, who is committed to the different task of bringing God's blessing into the material world. In order to accomplish that task he must make his peace with corporeal existence by accepting the *mizvot*. The *mizvot* thus serve to validate or legitimize corporeal existence itself. This line of thinking is, as we shall see, much more fully developed in the ḤaBaD sources, though there it takes a somewhat different turn.

The discussion to this point has hopefully made it clear that evidence of a struggle between the values of the spiritual life and the worldliness of *halakhah* is to be seen in the sources of Hasidism as they give rather frequent attention to the first patriarch and his relationship to the Law. Of course the option of claiming, as Paul once had, that Abraham stood entirely outside the Law was closed to them, both because of the talmudic dictum with which they had to work and their own commitment to post-rabbinic Jewish orthodoxy. Given these seemingly rigidly defined perimeters, the Hasidic authors show surprising flexibility in the range of their spiritualized readings of the matter. But perhaps we should not be *too* surprised at this near-flirtation with heresy. Hasidism is, after all, like early Christianity, a movement of spiritualist revival against the background of the religion of Hebrew Scripture. Each in its own way had to struggle with issues of law and spirit. We might even expect that both would light upon the figure of Abraham, living as he did before Sinai, and make him a focus of this discussion. What is more surprising is the fact that the discussion in Hasidism is not a new one, but is fully anticipated in the sources of medieval Judaism, where we might less expect it. The Hasidic sources, here as in all matters, draw richly on the body of lore that had come before them, bringing into explicit discussion that which had previously been indicated only by a hint.

III

Eastern European Hasidism is the epitome of what was once referred to in scholarly circles as *Spätjudentum*. Indeed, the movement's writings are filled with concern about having arrived so late on the scene of Jewish history. This anxiety usually manifests itself in mumbled apologies about the need to interpret Torah in such a way that it will have meaning "in every place and in every time." But while the major writings of Hasidism were composed a millennium and a half after the Midrashic classics, they remain faithful to the literary presuppositions that governed Jewish creativity throughout the many intervening centuries: the veracity of Scripture, the authority of *halakhah*, and, most significantly for our purposes, the truth-value of aggadic tradition, however reinterpreted. In this sense Hasidic thought still belongs to the classic rabbinic worldview. It is, in fact, the last major link in the chain of Jewish tradition of which this may be said unequivocally. Though from a socio-historical point of view Hasidism has rightly been depicted as a quasi-modern movement, reacting, as was *haskalah*, to the weakening of normative communal authority,[51] in an intellectual and spiritual sense Hasidism still belongs to the world that preceded it. Our purpose in this chapter is to seek out the earlier roots of the Hasidic treatment of Abraham and the commandments, thereby setting the Hasidic discussion in its proper historical and literary context.

The depiction of "Abraham our Father" as the embodiment of the life of piety has a remarkably long and consistent history within Judaism. Among the ideal types the tradition had to offer, it is especially the quality of devotion with which the first patriarch is associated. Moses was the "Master of all Prophets" and came closest to God in the revelation he received and in the intimacy of a face-to-face relationship. Other figures, including Adam before the fall, Jacob, and the still-anticipated messiah are occasionally spoken of in terms of greater godlike radiance than any other human being. David represents kingship as well as the Psalmist's longing for God, and Solomon embodies wisdom. Abraham remains for the Hasidic masters in the nineteenth century precisely what he was for Philo of Alexandria almost two thousand years before them: the ideal devotee. For preachers of all stripes along the way, including Midrashic authors, philosophers, and Kabbalists, the life of the patriarch was that which most clearly fulfilled the injunction to "know Him in all your ways."

In this context, the claim that Abraham lived in accord with the divine commandments is of course an ancient one. While it was clear that Abraham had lived prior to the Sinaitic revelation and thus before the formal acceptance of the Law, it would have seemed absurd to the Jewish pietist of any age to depict an Abraham who transgressed the Law as it was later known. It may even be that the surprisingly formulaic quality of Genesis 26:5 already reflects this tendency. We might expect an Abraham who "hearkened to My voice and kept My guard" as faithful to the narratives of the preceding chapters. But the added "My commandments, statutes, and teachings" seems reminiscent of such passages as Exodus 24:12 ("the stone tablets and the teaching and commandment") . . . and several in Deuteronomy, suggesting the voice of an inner biblical editor who already wanted to associate Abraham with the institutionalized forms of later biblical religion.[52]

The extra-biblical witness to a law-observing Abraham is also both early and unambiguous. Whatever ancient tradition is reflected in the Book of Jubilees already knows an Abraham who lived in accordance with the commandments, in a specific sense. Jubilees 12:27 is the earliest reference we have to an Abraham who studies "the books of his fathers," referring to the tradition well known to later Midrashic authors that Torah in some form was handed down from Adam through Methuselah, Shem, and Eber to Abraham. Jubilees (15:1ff; 16:21ff) also dates the festivals to the time of Abraham, as well as a host of other laws and practices, including a number related to the sacrificial cult. The presence of these references in second-century B.C.E. Jubilees and elsewhere in pre-Christian sources[53] makes it clear that the tradition of Abrahamic observance antedates Christianity and the rabbinic anti-Pauline polemic. It may indeed have been the background against which Paul's own views of Abraham were formed.

By far the most thorough and extensive ancient discussion of Abraham in extra-biblical sources is that to be found in the writings of Philo. Two treatises in the Philonic corpus, *De Abrahamo* and *De Migratione Abrahami*, deal wholly with the life and spirit of the patriarch,[54] but the figure of Abraham is a prominent one throughout the writings of Philo. The Philonic Abraham is the subject of an important monograph-length study by Samuel Sandmel, who uses the accounts of Abraham as a testing-ground with respect to the dependence of Philo on extra-biblical Palestinian Jewish traditions.[55]

The chief religious virtues which Abraham embodies for Philo are those of piety and faith. While Abraham the mystical philosopher is also the possessor of wisdom, and Abraham the ideal man in relation to other humans also represents the virtues of justice, courage, and self-control, it is primarily as a man of piety (*eu sebeia* or *theo sebeia*) that the patriarch is known. As such he is ever obedient to the will of God, a quality seen throughout his life, but most dramatically in his willingness to bind his son to the altar.[56] His trust in God is the highest of virtues, representing as it does a turn from the perceptible world and its vanities toward the intelligible and its unchanging truth.[57]

Since obedience plays such a central role in the life of piety, it would seem at first glance fair to say that Philo knows an Abraham who lived in accordance with the Law. A more careful reading, however, makes it clear that the law to which Abraham is obedient is the *unwritten* law, none other than the supreme law of nature. In fact, part of Philo's subtitle for *De Abrahamo* is "The First Book on Unwritten Laws." Abraham as a man of true virtue lives in absolute harmony with this law of nature, so much so that he himself may be called a law, one which itself can later be imitated in legislative form by the Law of Moses. Sandmel summarizes his views on the subject as follows:

> For Philo, as for Paul and the Rabbis, a fundamental problem regarding Abraham is the relationship between Abraham, the ancestor, and the descendant, Moses, and his Law. If Moses' Law was divine Law, how could Abraham (and the other patriarchs) have flourished without it? The Rabbis solve the problem in their way by asserting that Abraham observed the Mosaic Law; in fact, Abraham observed the Oral Law also. Paul is caught in the dilemma of a repudiation of the Mosaic Law and some defense of it; his solution is to regard the Law as having only temporary validity, beginning long after Abraham, who did not observe it, and enduring until Jesus, at which time it was abrogated. Philo gives his own answer, an answer possible only in Greek and not in rabbinic thinking: Abraham observed the law of nature and Abraham was himself a law; the Law of Moses is the copy of the law of nature, and the Law of Moses derives its specifications from those specific things which Abraham (and the other patriarchs) did.[58]

The figure of Abraham is important as a paradigm of piety, Philo says,

> because it demonstrates to us that those who wish to live in accordance with the laws as they stand have no difficult task, seeing as the first generations before any at all of the particular statutes was set in writing followed the unwritten law with perfect ease, so that one might properly say that the enacted laws are nothing else than memorials of the life of the ancients, preserving to a later generation their actual words and deeds.[59]

Abraham's conformity to this law is in a sense not commanded, but rather learned from within. Pious Abraham is zealous to follow God; he wants to obey the divine commands. These commands, Philo insists, are not such as are conveyed in speech and writing; they are those made manifest by nature and apprehended by the sense which is superior to hearing: sight or contemplation. Anyone who contemplates the order in nature and the constitution of the cosmos needs no teacher.[60] Here Philo's view differs interestingly from the Jubilees tradition that has Abraham learning wisdom from the writings passed down by his ancestors.

Philo's interpretation of Genesis 26:5, the passage used by the Rabbis to "prove" Abraham's observance of the Law, has Abraham living in accord with divine reason.[61] He does emphasize, however, that the allegorical figure of Abraham is not to be used to denigrate literal fulfillment of the Law in our own post-Mosaic times. Philo is of course quite aware of the distinction between literal and symbolic or allegorical understandings of the Law, and knows to separate "outward observances" from their "inner meanings."[62] He struggles to maintain a sense of proper balance between these two, implying in the course of polemical discussion that there are Jews in his time, presumably in Alexandria, who reveal a tendency to ignore literal performance of the commandments in favor of the claim that they have already absorbed the true meaning associated with the biblical statutes. It also seems likely, from the context of the polemic in *De Migratione Abrahami*, that these Jews used the figure of Abraham to justify their approach. While Philo's literal (or historical) Abraham was indeed one who lived in accord with the unwritten rather than any written law, our post-Mosaic way of access to the piety of Abraham is by following the path of his life as it was codified in the Law as we have received it.

The most important early treatment of Abraham and the Law, from the viewpoint of later historical developments, is of course that of Paul, the first great theologian of Christianity, whose position on the Law played a major role in the decisive break between the Jewish and Christian communities. Scholars of the New Testament are divided on the question of whether Paul was aware of the developments described above in non-Palestinian

Judaism or whether there were pre-Christian parallels within *Erez Yisrael* to the understandings of Abraham to be found in Philo's Alexandrian-Jewish milieu.[63] The use of Abraham as a figure who stands for a religious life that is not defined by law thus may or may not be original with him. There is no question, however, that the radical opposition proposed by Paul between law and both "faith" and "life" is indeed original. The very core of Paul's experience as a convert tells him that it is only through faith in Jesus as the Christ that true "life" can be found. The Jewish, and specifically the Pharisaic, attempt to see Torah as a source of such life is doomed to failure. Faith in Christ sets one free from "enslavement" to the Law, which itself does not rest on faith, the only true source of righteousness. The motif of vain bondage to law and faith in Christ as liberation from that bondage is most strongly expressed in Galatians 3:2–3:

> Let me ask you only this: Did you receive the Spirit by works of the Law, or by hearing with faith? Are you so foolish? Having begun with the Spirit, are you now ending with the flesh?

The apostle to the gentiles insists that there is but a single source of salvation for all, Jew and gentile alike, in the acceptance of faith in Christ. While he may not seek to prevent Jewish Christians from continuing to live according to the Law, he deems their doing so as irrelevant to their salvation, and he severely warns gentile Christians to avoid entry into the domain of the Law, which is seen as a vain but nonetheless rival claimant to the mantle of salvation.[64]

The major sources for Paul's discussion of the Law are to be found in Galatians 2–3, Philippians 3, II Corinthians 3:7–11, and Romans 4–10. In the course of these discussions, Paul refers several times to Abraham as one who lived in faith before the Law was given and outside its domain. Genesis 15:6, "Abraham trusted in the Lord, and He considered that for him as righteousness," a central proof-text for Paul, occurs in the scriptural narrative prior to the account of Abraham's circumcision; Paul notes (Romans 4:11) that "consequently, he is the father of all who have faith when uncircumcised." He goes on to say that "it was not through law that Abraham, or his posterity, was given the promise that the world should be his inheritance, but through the righteousness that came through faith" (v. 13). In a daring bit of allegorical *midrash*, Paul claims in Galatians 4:21ff. that the Christian in faith is the true son of Abraham through the line of Isaac, while those who remain bound to the Law are "the slave-woman's son," spiritually descended through Hagar and Ishmael.

Paul's arguments were known and used against Judaism by Christian polemicists throughout the ages, beginning as early as Justin Martyr's *Contra Trypho*, in which much is made of the Jew's admission that Abraham and the other righteous who lived before Sinai have achieved salvation, presumably without need for the Law.[65] Interestingly, the Jew here does not make use of those traditions, presumably well-known in second-century Palestine, which claimed that Abraham did in fact observe the Law. However, Justin may be looking for an easy foil and not wanting to complicate the discussion in a propagandistic work.

It is in this polemical context that the rabbinic insistence on Abraham's full observance of the Torah must be seen.[66] As I have indicated above, these passages are in one sense a part of the broader effort to convert all the heroes of biblical Israel into observant and scholarly rabbinic Jews. But the frequency with which the claims regarding Abraham appear and the directness with which they are phrased indicate that something more is at work here. Other figures are made into proto-Rabbis in the course of exegesis or for some specified homiletical reason; only of Abraham do the Rabbis state flatly that "he fulfilled the entire Torah." While the tradition reflected as early as Jubilees was surely formative here, this sort of absolute assertion is not made before Tannaitic times, when the Christian use of Abraham was already well known. The image of a Torah-observant Abraham did not originate in response to Christianity—indeed, we have seen traces of it in pre-Christian sources—but the need arose for its bold assertion in the wake of Christian claims.

A single Mishnaic source constitutes our earliest testimony to this rabbinic belief. Qiddushin 4:14 tells us

> We find that Abraham our father performed the entire Torah before
> it was given, as Scripture says: "Because Abraham listened to My
> voice," etc.

It is interesting to note that the earliest witness already ties this
claim to the exegesis of a biblical verse (Gen. 26:5), a somewhat
unusual practice for the Mishnah. An expanded version of this
statement, found in Tosefta Qiddushin 5, clarifies the precise
exegetical point being made:

> The Ever-present blessed him in his old age more than in his youth.
> Why so much? Because he performed the Torah before it came [into
> the world], as Scripture says: "Because Abraham listened to My
> voice." It does not say "My teaching" [*torati*], but rather "My teach-
> ings" [*torotay*], indicating that the meanings of Torah and its details
> were revealed to him.

A more straightforward understanding of the plural in *torotay* is
preserved in the alternative reading of the Erfurt manuscript of
the Tosefta: "The words of Torah and the words of the scribes
were revealed to him."[67] The term *niglu*, "were revealed," is
noteworthy in this context, though I do not share Urbach's certi-
tude that it indicates that Abraham did not learn Torah from
within himself.[68] Another version of this tradition, current at least
from early Amoraic times, seeks to demonstrate that Abraham
fulfilled "the words of the scribes" by offering an example of a
practice that had no scriptural basis. Hence the mention of *'eruv
tavshilin* in the passage from Yoma quoted above, or the alternative
'eruvey hazerot found in other versions.[69]

Various other passages in rabbinic literature apply the notion
of patriarchal observance of the commandments in a more
"natural" way, in the course of the Midrashic expansion of the
biblical narrative. Thus we learn that Abraham ate his ordinary
food in a state of ritual purity, that Jacob observed the Sabbath,
and so forth.[70] The problem of Jacob's marrying two sisters, in
clear violation of the Levitical prohibition, which so vexed some
of the medieval commentators, does not seem to have bothered
the early Rabbis.[71] The principle that "there are no 'earlier' and
'later' in the Torah" was taken to the extreme when the Rabbis

said that Joseph was taken from Jacob while they were studying the law of the broken-necked heifer, and that the long-lost son signaled his identity to his bereaved father by sending him wagons (Gen. 45:21), playing on the linguistic similarity of 'eglah and 'agalot.

The question of how Abraham came to know Torah also occurs in rabbinic sources. Typically for the aggadic worldview, no distinction whatever is made between Abraham's knowledge of Torah and his discovery of God. The same passage in Bereshit Rabbah that tells of Joseph's signal to his father continues:

> . . . to teach you that wherever he went he studied Torah, as had his forefathers. But the Torah had not yet been given! Scripture says of Abraham, however, "He kept My guard" (Gen. 26:5). Whence did Abraham learn Torah? Rabbi Simeon ben Yohai said: His two kidneys became like two pitchers flowing with Torah. Whence [do we learn] this? Scripture says: "I will bless the Lord who has counselled me, in the night my kidneys have instructed me" (Ps. 16:1). Rabbi Levi says: He learned Torah from himself, as Scripture says: "The renegade reaps the fruit of his conduct, a good man the fruit of his own" (Prov. 14:14). Rabbi Samuel ben Nahmani said in the name of Rabbi Jonathan ben Eleazar of Sepphoris: Abraham knew even 'eruvey tavshilin, as it says: "Because Abraham listened to My voice," etc. [apparently referring to torotay, as above]. How old was Abraham when he came to know his Creator? Rabbi Hananya said: He was one year old. Rabbi Levi said in the name of Rabbi Simeon ben Lakish: He was three years old, for it says 'eqev ["because"]. The numerical value of 'eqev is 172, and Abraham lived 175 years. Thus he was three years old when he came to know his Creator. He kept even the fine points of Torah and he taught Torah to his children, as it says: "For I have known him so that he command his children and his household after him that they guard the way of the Lord." (Gen. 18:19).[72]

This important text combines a number of elements that are found separately elsewhere. The question of whether Abraham first learned of God from books or from within himself may reflect an ancient theological debate, the context of which is now lost to us. The text as we have it fully integrates the traditions concerning Abraham's knowledge of Torah with those discussing his acknowledgment of God.[73] Most interestingly, the statements concerning his learning Torah from within himself are found elsewhere in answer to the question, "Whence did Abraham come to know his Creator?" The Rabbis have responded unequivocally: faith in God and knowledge of Torah were as inseparable for the patriarch as they are for his descendants.

A discordant note in this seeming rabbinic unanimity regarding Abraham and the Torah is recorded in the final text we must consider before moving on to the medieval sources. In introducing his praises of the revelation at Sinai, R. Judah ben Simon recounts earlier revelations of the commandments: "Adam was given seven commandments . . . Noah was commanded concerning the limbs of living animals . . . Abraham concerning circumcision" and so forth. Here the plain meaning of Scripture, at least in Abraham's case, seems to be followed. But not too much should be made of this text, the point of which is to say of Moses, "But you have excelled above them all" (Prov. 3:29). Aggadic claims could after all be set aside when the homiletic point was best made without them. Or it may be that Abraham *observed* the entire Torah but was actually only *commanded* concerning circumcision, the rest of observance coming more as a free-will offering. This same text goes on, however, to provide us with another important building block used in construction of the Hasidic homilies with which we began. Referring to Moses or Israel, it says:

> But you at Sinai were given 613 commandments, 248 requirements and 365 prohibitions. The 248 positive commandments parallel the 248 human limbs. Each limb entreats the person, saying: "Please perform this commandment with me." The 365 negative commandments parallel the 365 days of the solar year, each day saying to the person: "Please do not perform this transgression on me."[74]

While the Midrash here explicitly excludes Abraham from such awareness, assigning the 613 commandments only to Sinai, it is easy to see how the later mythic consciousness ignored this distinction and combined the rabbinic tradition that Abraham learned Torah from within himself with this account of the limbs calling out for fulfillment of the commandments. But even that combination, as we shall see, very much antedates Levi Yizhak of Berdichev.

IV

The recasting of Judaism into philosophical language that took place during the early Middle Ages brought with it, as might be expected, new understandings of the ideal figure of biblical piety. Philosopher and exegete worked hand in hand to portray an Abraham who embodied the virtues of rationality, sobriety, and discipline that were so highly prized by the Jewish elite of those times. In this process of recasting, certain elements of the rabbinic *aggadah* were found attractive and were widely used, while others were not. Most impressive to the medievals must have been the traditions that Abraham discovered God from within himself or on his own initiative. Both the *aggadah* that showed Abraham turning inward and that which traced progressive stages whereby the patriarch worshipped sun and moon, only to discover that God must be beyond them both, served beautifully to justify the role of independent philosophical investigation in the quest for religious truth.[75]

Probably best known among the medieval portrayals of the patriarchs is that by Maimonides in the *Guide for the Perplexed*. Making no distinction between Moses and the patriarchs for this purpose, Maimonides describes these four as the ideal examples of the pious life:

> And there may be a human individual who, through his apprehension of the true realities and his joy in what he has apprehended, achieves a state in which he talks with people and is occupied with his bodily necessities while his intellect is wholly turned toward Him, may He be exalted, so that in his heart he is always in His presence, may He be exalted, while outwardly he is with people, in the sort of way described by the poetical parables that have been invented for these notions: "I sleep, but my heart waketh; it is the voice of my beloved that knocketh," and so on. I do not say that this rank is that of all the prophets; but I do say that this is the rank of Moses our Master, of whom it is said: "And Moses alone shall come near unto the Lord; but they shall not come near"; and of whom it is said: "And he was there with the Lord"; and to whom it was said:

"But as for thee, stand thou here by Me." All this according to what
we have explained regarding the meaning of these verses. This was
also the rank of the Patriarchs, the result of whose nearness to Him,
may He be exalted, was that His name became known to the world
through them: "The God of Abraham, the God of Isaac, and the
God of Jacob . . . : this is My name for ever." Because of the union
of their intellects through apprehension of Him, it came about that
He made a lasting covenant with each of them: "Then I will re-
member My covenant with Jacob," and so on. For in those four, I
mean the Patriarchs and Moses our Master, union with God—I
mean apprehension of Him and love of Him—became manifest, as
the texts testify. Also the providence of God watching over them
and over their posterity was great. Withal they were occupied with
governing people, increasing their fortune, and endeavoring to
acquire property. Now this is to my mind a proof that they performed
these actions with their limbs only, while their intellects were constantly in His presence, may He be exalted. It also seems to me that
the fact that these four were in a permanent state of extreme perfection in the eyes of God, and that His providence watched over
them continually even while they were engaged in increasing their
fortune—I mean while they tended their cattle, did agricultural
work, and governed their household—was necessarily brought about
by the circumstance that in all these actions their end was to come
near to Him, may He be exalted; and how near! For the end of their
efforts during their life was to bring into being a religious community that would know and worship God. "For I have known him,
to the end that he may command," and so on. Thus it has become
clear to you that the end of all their efforts was to spread the doctrine
of the *unity of the Name in the world* and to guide people to love Him,
may He be exalted.[76]

While there is no mention, either positive or negative, of the role
of commandments in the life of piety described here, it seems fair
to say that the greatest of Jewish philosophers does not make use
here of the tradition of patriarchal observance of the *mizvot*. These
four great figures of piety are able to remain attached to God
while involved in ordinary human acts of conversation, occupation
with bodily needs, and the pursuit of a livelihood. It was of their
concentration of mind and the intensity of their love for God that
their greatness consisted. It was their "nearness" to Him that
caused His name to be known throughout the world. In the case

of Abraham, this nearness had already been discussed in *Guide* 3:24, where the first patriarch is described at length as the ideal of piety and the embodiment of deliberate, intelligent fear of God for his actions at Mount Moriah.

> For in this story he [Abraham] was ordered to do something that bears no comparison either with sacrifice of property or with sacrifice of life. In truth it is the most extraordinary thing that could happen in the world, such a thing that one would not imagine that human nature was capable of it. Here there is a sterile man having an exceeding desire for a son, possessed of great property and commanding respect, and having the wish that his progeny should become a religious community. When a son comes to him after his having lost hope, how great will be his attachment to him and love for him! However, because of his fear of Him, who should be exalted, and because of his love to carry out His command, he holds this beloved son as little, gives up all his hopes regarding him, and hastens to slaughter him after a journey of days. For if he had chosen to do this immediately, as soon as the order came to him, it would have been an act of stupefaction and disturbance in the absence of exhaustive reflection. But his doing it days after the command had come to him shows that the act sprang from thought, correct understanding, consideration of the truth of His command, may He be exalted, love of Him, and fear of Him. . . .
>
> In truth it was fitting that this story, I mean the binding, should come to pass through the hand of Abraham and in regard to someone like Isaac. For Abraham our Father was the first to make known the belief in Unity, to establish prophecy, and to perpetuate this opinion and draw people to it.

The *'aqedah* is depicted here as the epitome of faith, the highest example imaginable of human willingness to follow the command of God and to demonstrate love and fear of the Divine. This lofty picture of ideal devotion to God does not need the support of the assertion that the patriarch kept the Mosaic commandments. Abraham's affirmation, it would seem, was on another level, one that lends meaning to fulfillment of the divine command for his descendants in all generations.

The view of Abraham as an ideal figure of intense but philosophic piety was widespread in the Jewish Middle Ages. For Joseph ibn Caspi, writing in early fourteenth-century Spain, Abraham was a contemplative philosopher of the Aristotelian school, much as he had earlier been a Hellenistic philosopher and mystic for the sage of Alexandria:

> Truth burned like a fire in the heart of our father Abraham. I refer to that which he apprehended in knowledge of the existence of God, blessed be He, namely the separate intellect, which is higher even than the intellect that moves the uppermost sphere.

The notion that Abraham kept the entire Torah was among those *aggadot* which did not fare well in the Middle Ages before the advent of Kabbalah. The new emphasis on the plain meaning of Scripture led interpreters away from this extravagant violation of the biblical text. Saadya's translation of the Torah already notes (Genesis 26:5) that Abraham observed "all that I commanded him to keep of my commandments," a subtly worded rejection of the rabbinic *aggadah*. [78] Judah ben Barzilai of Barcelona, in his twelfth-century commentary on *Sefer Yezirah*, emphasizes that Abraham fulfilled the pre-existent Torah by means of the single commandment of circumcision, "which is as weighty as the entire Torah." [79] The point is made more sharply by Abraham ibn Ezra, who says that "My commandments" in this verse refers to the commandments to Abraham to leave his father's house and to offer up his son. "My statutes" indicates that "a person should follow His deeds," and, Ibn Ezra adds, "These statutes are implanted in the heart." "My teachings" shows that "he circumcised himself, his sons, and his servants." Ibn Ezra has found a reading of the verse, in all its detail, that does not do violence to the biblical narrative. Elsewhere Ibn Ezra makes it clear that *huqqot* for him are the inviolable laws of nature as God has established them, rather than unexplained ritual laws of the Torah. "These," he says, "are implanted in the heart," or, in another passage, "were known by intellectual process before the Torah was given through Moses." [80]

The commentary of David Kimchi on Genesis 26:5 is also quite explicit in seeking an alternative to the rabbinic understanding of this passage. Kimchi claims that Abraham observed "all of the rational commandments, both the well-known and the obscure." He adds that

among the seven Noachide commandments there are matters the
reasons for which are revealed only to the sages. These include the
[prohibitions of] the mixed breeding of animals, the grafting of trees,
and eating the limb of a living animal. That is why it says "My
statutes." "My commandments" refers to the totality of rational
commandments, those involving the heart, the hand, and the mouth,
both positive and negative.

This original comment in fact typifies an interesting mix of *peshaṭ*
and rabbinic tradition. The idea of Abraham's observance of the
entire Torah is seemingly offensive to the rational mind of the
exegete, doing violence as it does to the chronological sequence
of Scripture. But the alternative proposed is itself based on a
combination of rabbinic assertions which themselves have no real
scriptural base. Kimchi accepts the tradition of seven Noachide
commandments as well as the rabbinic designation of *hoq* ("statute")
as referring to an unexplained ritual practice. In order to justify
the presence of *huqqim* ("statutes") in the list of that which Abraham
observed, without recourse to the extravagance of the rabbinic
claim, Kimchi offers examples of *huqqim* that were to be found
among the Noachide commandments! Kimchi goes on to mention
the aggadic claim, even offering an interpretation of why *'eruv
tavshilin* was selected as an example, but he distances this quotation
from his actual interpretation of the verse. Of the early commentators, only RaSHI remains fully faithful to the rabbinic understanding of the verse.

This Abraham of the medieval rationalists, expressing his
unfailing devotion to God through meticulous observance of
the Noachide commandments and circumcision, is reminiscent
of the Philonic Abraham. Once again, as in Philo's Alexandria,
we see that a changed intellectual setting has brought about
a new biography of the patriarch. The law he observes is not
quite the "natural" law of Philo, but it is a combination of the
universally ordained Noachide law, which is as close as
medieval Judaism comes to a concept of "natural law," and
the "rational commandments," those of the non-Noachide
Torah laws that could be discovered by the efforts of the
norm-seeking rational mind.

It was among the earliest Kabbalistic commentators that a further development in the figure of Abraham took place, one that set the stage for the later Hasidic readings. Such figures as Nahmanides and Bahya ben Asher, through whose influence the contemplative Abraham of the Middle Ages reached the latter-day Hasidic authors, combine a shared sense of the medieval contemplative ideal[81] with a greater need than that of the rationalists to justify rabbinic *aggadah* and to integrate it into their own reading of Scripture. Indeed, it was often those very aggadic statements which had offended the rationalists that gave rise to the innovations in symbolic language which lie at the heart of Kabbalistic creativity. In the writings of these thinkers, the Abraham who observed the entire Torah is combined with Abraham the spiritual seeker, and no tension between these becomes apparent.

Nahmanides' comment on Genesis 26:5 demonstrates his desire to keep faith with both traditions. He begins by quoting RaSHI in full, offering a traditional rabbinic reading of the verse. To this he raises a series of objections. If the patriarchs observed the entire Torah, he asks,

> How could Jacob have erected a stone monument and married two sisters, or four, according to the rabbis? And how could Amram have married his aunt? Or Moses set up twelve stone monuments? How could they have permitted these things if their father Abraham had forbidden them to himself, for which God had rewarded him? [Had he not] commanded his children and his household to follow in his ways?

Nahmanides then offers an alternative reading, based on the method of Ibn Ezra, in which Abraham is seen to keep only the Noachide precepts. Finally he proposes his own opinion, divided in two parts. "That which appears [correct] to me of our Rabbis' opinion," he says, is that

> Abraham our father learned the entire Torah in the holy spirit and concerned himself with the meanings of its commandments and its secrets. He kept it all, but as one who is not commanded to do so. He kept it only while in the Land, and it was outside the Land that

> Jacob was wed to two sisters, and the same with Amram. The
> commandments are the judgment of the God of the Land.

Two important innovations are offered here. The distinction
between Abraham's *knowledge* of the entire Torah and his *obligation*
to fulfill it is a subtle but crucial one. For Nahmanides the Kabbalist, the ancient notion of primordial Torah has a major role to
play. We will recall the famous introduction to his Torah commentary in which he claims that the original Torah has an alternative form that is nought but the great mysterious name of God.
The Torah as given at Sinai is divided into words and commandments; Torah before Sinai was written "with letters of black fire
upon a background of white fire" and seemingly was not yet
divided into words.[82] The Torah Abraham studied, then, is the
mystical Torah. The "holy spirit" apparently gave him sufficient
foretaste of the Torah's Mosaic version to allow him to contemplate
ta'amey hamizvot (the reasons for the commandments). But these
were not yet commanded to him; he naturally observed them,
but only on a voluntary basis. He furthermore did so only while
in the Land of Israel, a uniquely Nahmanidean theme that we
have seen reflected in a homily of Levi Yizhak of Berdichev.
Nahmanides does not link non-observance outside the Land with
the impossibility there of observing Torah in its entirety, but says
rather tersely that Torah embodies "the judgements of the God
of the Land."

   After resolving the other difficulties he had raised, he goes on
to offer an explanation in the straightforward manner.

> "My guard" refers to faith in God, for Abraham believed in the
> Name of Unity. He kept this guard in his heart and argued with
> idolators over it. He called upon the name of the Lord to bring
> many to His service. "My commandments" means all that God
> had commanded him, including going forth from his land, offering
> his son, and the expulsion of his handmaiden and her son. "My
> statutes": walking in the ways of the Lord, being merciful and
> compassionate, doing justice and law, and commanding his sons
> and household to do the same. "My teachings": circumcising himself,
> his sons, and his servants, and all the laws of Noah, for these were
> Torah for them.

Nahmanides' "straightforward" explanation belongs entirely to the school of thought expressed by Ibn Ezra and Kimchi. He does no more to choose between these two very different readings of the verse; clearly both represented truth for him. So long as the "truth" represented in the rabbinic sources and that brought about by the "straightforward" reading were not directly in conflict with one another, Nahmanides was able to hold fast to both.[83]

Nahmanides' follower Bahya, however, is apparently discomforted by the unresolved contradiction in his master's reading. That which Nahmanides had found true in the rabbinic reading convinced him to say that Abraham did keep the Mosaic commandments, if only on a voluntary basis. The "straightforward" reading, however, seems to leave no room for such a claim. It is for this reason that Bahya adds a single crucial word to his comment on the rabbinic claim. Abraham our Father, according to the Rabbis, "observed the entire Torah *be-sekhel* (in his mind)." Thus the conflict is resolved: *contemplatively* Abraham "observed" all the commandments, but *in practice* he observed only those that applied in his time. Here the view expressed by Nahmanides is carried a short but critical step further. RaMBaN depicted an Abraham who was able to *study* the esoteric reasons for all the commandments, including those which he had not yet been enjoined to follow in practice. Bahya uses this view as a way of understanding the rabbinic claim that he had *observed* them, a claim now so difficult to uphold in the face of medieval *peshat* exegesis. The conclusion must have been an obvious one to him: the contemplation of the commandments *is* their fulfillment on an intellectual level; it is this to which the Rabbis referred when they said that "Abraham our Father fulfilled the entire Torah."[84]

For the Kabbalists, themselves claimants to a supposedly ancient tradition of esoteric wisdom, it was the fact that Abraham had received or discovered the Torah that was the crucial part of the rabbinic claim. Thus was the Torah of Israel—including its esoteric meaning—tied to the "original" Torah existent prior to Creation and known to Adam. On the lesser question of actual observance, they were seemingly more ready to concede. Isaac of Acre, writing in Spain at the turn of the fourteenth century, writes of the Covenant in Genesis 15:

> Perhaps in this hour Abraham our Father reached the knowledge of God's commanded statutes and His teachings just as Israel attained to them at Mount Sinai when the Torah was given. Of this Scripture says: "He kept My guard, statutes, commandments, and teachings." If he did not receive them from the *shekhinah*, from whom did he receive them? And if not now, when? This receiving was his donning of the holy spirit, so that his kidneys flowed like a font [of wisdom].[85]

Note that our verse is here interpreted without any reference to observance at all; it is the *revelation*, described as coming both from the *shekhinah* and from Abraham's innards, that has taken center stage.

One further passage from Bahya again illustrates this circle's disinterest in pressing the point of patriarchal observance. In his comment on Exodus 20:9, regarding the prohibition of Sabbath labor, Bahya briefly mentions that

> On all six days it is possible to serve God with the doing of your labors, just as the patriarchs served God through working with their flocks and in other material ways.[86]

The image of the patriarchs' devotional life here called to mind is based on Maimonides' view and is hardly that of meticulous observance of rabbinic law. In fact we have in this passage a basis for the view we have seen in Hasidism that the patriarchs fulfilled what we do in the commandments by other deeds of their own.

Nahmanides' image of an Abraham who observed the entire Torah out of desire rather than in response to command calls to mind another aspect of the Kabbalistic Abraham, a figure who differs considerably from the Abraham of the philosophers. For the Kabbalist, each of the patriarchs is symbolically associated with one of the *sefirot* or stages in the unfolding of the divine persona. Just as Philo's Abraham functioned on both literal and allegorical levels, the Zohar's Abraham is both a figure in human history and a rung within divinity. The earliest Kabbalistic source known to us, *Sefer ha-Bahir*, identifies Abraham with *ḥesed* (divine "love" or "grace") within the sefirotic world. Again quoting Genesis 26:5, the Bahir text reads:

> The quality of *ḥesed* said before the Blessed Holy One: So long as Abraham was in the world, I did not have to do anything, as Scripture says: "He kept My guard."[87]

The historic Abraham becomes the symbol of *ḥesed* because he fully realized *ḥesed* in his life. *Ḥesed*, the right side of the divine "body," represents the free and unrestricted gift of love, not yet balanced by the limiting and judging forces of the left. It is no wonder that the Abraham who represents this aspect of divine and human personality chooses to fulfill the Torah out of desire, without legal obligation. While "love" and "law" are certainly not opposed in the Kabbalistic mind the way they are in Paul, the Kabbalists' Abraham is a figure especially befitting this devotional image of the religious life as an undemanded free-will offering to God. Nahmanides' assertion that Abraham observed the Torah without being commanded to do so is not merely an exegetical convenience, but an understanding of the patriarch that well fits the Kabbalistic imagination.

This Kabbalistic Abraham, a man devoted wholly to the quality of *ḥesed*, is quite thoroughly combined with the philosophers' Abraham in the following passage from Joseph Gikatilla's *Sha'arey Orah*, a Castilian introduction to Kabbalah composed in the late thirteenth century:

> When Abraham our Father, peace be upon him, arrived, he looked and saw, investigated and understood the great secret of the blessed God and how He had created the world through the attribute of *ḥesed*. He too then held fast to this quality. He saw all the people of the world enraptured with idolatry, each one cleaving to his own particular heathen form. Then Abraham our Father, peace be upon him, rose up and announced to everyone that "'all the gods of the nations are false gods, but the Lord has made the heavens' (Ps. 96:6). Know all you peoples there is a Creator who made and who alone rules all the worlds, who brings life and death, brings down to the nether world and raises up, lowers and uplifts." They rose up against

him, looted all his possessions, put him in prison, and cast him into
a fiery furnace. After he was saved from that furnace he was expelled
from his land and he sacrificed his wealth, his wife, and his family
for the sake of God's service. The quality of *hesed* calls out from above
concerning Abraham and says "I approached [or 'preceded'] the
world from the side of lovingkindness and I was alone in the world.
Now Abraham, alone in the world, approaches Me with *hesed*.
Abraham is fit to hold fast to Me, and I to him." Then Abraham
returned to *hesed* as an inheritance and it was given to him, as
Scripture says: "You give truth to Jacob, *hesed* to Abraham" (Micah
7:20). The meaning of the verse is thus: Know that Abraham our
Father, peace be upon him, performed the service of God without a
teacher or father to teach him and without God's sending any prophet
to chastise him or to warn him. He on his own looked and saw, in-
vestigated and understood until he entered into awareness of the
blessed Lord's sovereignty. Just as God had created the world through
hesed, so did Abraham know his Creator through *hesed*. [88]

Abraham the seeker after truth and Abraham the embodiment
of divine *hesed* are here combined. While Gikatilla does not refer
explicitly to the question of Abraham's observance of the Law,
his viewpoint seems to be the same as that of Nahmanides, expressed so as not to come into direct conflict with the talmudic
dictum. Abraham served God without need for instruction, and
especially without need of any prophecy, which is to say with no
need for revelation beyond that which he discovered from within
himself. Precisely of what this "service" of God consisted is not
detailed by Gikatilla.

The greatest compendium of medieval Kabbalistic thought, the
Zohar, contains a great deal of material on Abraham; here the
historical and symbolic Abraham are often fully conflated. A
certain amount of allegorical use of Abraham, clearly distinguishable from the symbolic, is found in the *Midrash ha-Ne'elam* stratum
of the Zohar literature, where Abraham stands for the soul and
Sarah the body.[89] Two views of Abraham's fulfillment of the
commandments are to be found in the Zohar. In the original work
by Moses de Leon, the more textually justifiable understanding
of this teaching is supported. Abraham in fact observed the single
mizvah of circumcision, but this one act was deemed to bear within
it the entire Torah:

> Whoever keeps this covenant is like unto one who keeps the entire Torah; one who betrays this is like one who betrays the entire Torah. Come and see: Before Abraham was circumcised, Scripture does not say that he kept the Torah. But once he was circumcised, what is written? "Because Abraham listened to My voice and kept My guard, My commandments, statutes, and teachings" (Gen. 26:5). All this because he was circumcised; a holy sign was impressed upon him and he kept it properly. It was thus considered as though he had kept the entire Torah.[90]

We might at first be surprised that the Zohar accepts the interpretation of our verse that is closer to the *peshaṭ* and seemingly less "rabbinic." But we should bear in mind that there is already justification for this view in the old rabbinic sources, as we have seen. It also happens that this reading fits in well with the religious psychology of Moses de Leon, author of the Zohar, who was obsessed with the need for sexual purity. It is the value of this homiletic usage, rather than a sympathy for the plain meaning of Scripture, that puts the Zohar on the side of Ibn Ezra in his understanding of our verse. Not surprisingly, the greatest of later Zohar commentators, Moses Cordovero (1522–1570), was unhappy with this passage, implying that Abraham kept only the one commandment. He interprets the Zohar to mean that

> as much as he occupied himself with the commandments, their lights were darkened by the "foreskin." Afterwards, when he was circumcised, it was as though his fulfillment of them was renewed, as he caused them to shine forth and awaken from the darkness that had covered them [lit.: "the darkness of their foreskin"].[91]

Cordovero's Abraham had apparently been living in accord with the Torah's commandments all along, but their true light shone only after he had been transformed by the act of the covenant. This view, too, seems to have ancient precedents.[92]

But the other view of Abraham's fulfillment of the *mizvot* is also to be found in the Zohar literature. The *Ra'aya Mehemna*, an addendum to de Leon's work composed by an anonymous Kabbalist around 1300 but always printed as a part of the Zohar, describes the patriarch as fulfilling the commandments through his daughter, the *shekhinah*. The Zohar here plays on an earlier rabbinic interpretation of Gen. 24:1 which claimed that "Abraham had a daughter whose name was *ba-kol* (lit.: "in all"). Kabbalistic tradition from the outset had made much of this *aggadah*, using it to trace a special relationship between *ḥesed* and *malkhut* or *shekhinah* within the sefirotic world. Gikatilla's work in particular favored this image, in which the historic Abraham, father of *ba-kol*, inherits or adopts the *shekhinah* as his own beloved "daughter" as well. It is because of this relationship to *shekhinah*, the source of all blessing, that Abraham himself becomes a fount of blessing in the world.[93] Now the *Ra'aya Mehemna*, a mystical work that generally evinces more interest in law than does de Leon's Zohar, uses this same image to claim that Abraham fulfilled all the commandments through this daughter. The prophet Elijah, often the conveyer of secrets in this work, says in one of his speeches to Moses:

> O faithful shepherd! This bride of yours was given to Abraham that he might raise her. Because he guarded her she was called his daughter, as it is written: "Abraham our Father had a daughter whose name was *ba-kol*." Through her he fulfilled the entire Torah, even *'eruvey tavshilin*, as Scripture says: "He kept My guard" etc. He was like a parent to her, as in, "He [Mordecai] was the foster-father of Hadassah" (Esth. 2:7). God blessed him because of her, as Scripture says: "And God blessed Abraham in all." (Gen. 24:1).[94]

The precise relationship of Abraham, *ḥesed*, *shekhinah*, and commandments is not clear in this passage. Is it out of fatherly concern that Abraham fulfills the commandments, instructing his adopted "daughter" as Mordecai taught his? Such a usage would be especially interesting, indicating that even in a social climate where religious instruction for daughters was minimal, the obligation was sufficiently powerful to serve this symbolic role. Or is it through the *shekhinah* in another sense that Abraham fulfills the commandments? This "daughter" of his is, after all, identified with the Oral Torah. It may be that by knowing the *shekhinah*, as he raised her, Abraham came to an awareness of all the commandments, including such as *'eruv tavshilin*, distinctly a part of the Oral Law alone. Thus the *Ra'aya Mehemna* could be seen as insisting that Abraham did fulfill all the *miẓvot*, not just that of the covenant.

He did so before revelation by coming to know the *shekhinah*, who herself embodies them all.

It would behoove us at this point to note that virtually all the building blocks of the later Hasidic homilies are in place in these early Kabbalistic sources which antedate Hasidism by some four hundred years. Bahya offers us contemplative (or "spiritual") fulfillment of the commandments. Nahmanides mentions observance only inside the Land. Several medieval exegetical sources, including the later, highly authoritative Zohar, suggest fulfillment of "My commandments" to refer to circumcision. The correspondence between limbs and *mizvot* has, as we have seen, an ancient history, which is taken up with some frequency in Kabbalistic writings.[95]

Preachers throughout the later generations, influenced by the images of Abraham in the medieval classics, dealt regularly with the question of the patriarch and the commandments, largely repeating positions already expressed. The discussion occasionally entered into Jewish polemical literature generated by the ongoing Jewish-Christian disputations of the Middle Ages.[96] Some devoted themselves to explaining why the Talmud had chosen the particular example of *'eruv tavshilin*;[97] others offered yet another combination of the philosophic and Kabbalistic readings. A particularly elegant summation of the medieval discussion, expressing a view essentially identical with that of Bahya, is to be found in the sixteenth-century homiletical work *Ma'asey ha-Shem* of Eliezer Ashkenazi.[98] None of these sources, however, frames the discussion as had Justin Martyr. Clearly the patriarchs had no lack of merit, with or without the commandments. The idea of an "unsaved" Abraham (or one without "a portion in the world to come") would have been an utter absurdity to Jews of any age.

We need to devote careful attention to one final pre-Hasidic text, which I believe to be the proximate source for the Hasidic discussions. Of the many devotional works composed in the sixteenth and seventeenth centuries, none exercised so great an influence upon Eastern European Jewry as the *Two Tablets of the Covenant* by Isaiah Horowitz of Prague.[99] The *SHeLaH ha-Qadosh*, as it was called, was a conduit for Kabbalistic thought and its transformation into the popular ethos of Hasidism. More than one supposedly "original" Hasidic homily or idea has been traced to this work. In the introduction to his Torah commentary, which forms the last part of this work, Horowitz goes into a lengthy disquisition on the 613 commandments. Since each of these corresponds to a limb or sinew of the spiritual body, a person must perform them all in order to attain wholeness. But such wholeness is impossible to achieve, he goes on to say. Not only do some commandments apply only to Temple times or in the Land of Israel, but the system itself does not allow any one person to fulfill them all, even in theory. Some commandments apply only to *kohanim*, others only to Levites, and still others only to ordinary Israelites! And other commandments are only occasional: Shall a happily married man have to divorce his wife in order to fulfill "he shall write her a bill of divorce?" In the course of this discussion Horowitz turns to the question of the commandments before Sinai:

> As soon as Adam was created, God gave him *mizvot,* as Scripture says: "The Lord God commanded the man," which the sages refer to the seven commandments that he was obliged to perform. All 613 commandments were included and hidden within these. Had they been obligated to do so, Adam, Methuselah, Enoch, Noah, Shem, Eber, the patriarchs, the tribes, and all the other righteous of the world [who lived] before the Torah was given would have fulfilled them. Israel was commanded to observe all 613 in order to be whole; even though each one in fact contains them all, they had to draw forth the potential that lay within them [performing them all] in deed. Might you then say that the patriarchs and the other righteous of early days did not fulfill their potential? Know that indeed they did so by the power of their preparedness. I mean to say that they were absolutely attached (*deveqim be-takhlit ha-devequt*) to the Creator, joyously ready to fulfill His will in whatever He might demand of them. They were absolutely prepared to do His bidding, in joy and goodheartedness. And this preparedness was tantamount to the deed itself. [100]

He goes on to tie this notion of devotional readiness on the part of the patriarchs to the legal prohibition of *preparing* for weekday work on the Sabbath or festival, the very matter covered by *'eruv tavshilin!* Though he does not say so explicitly, he undoubtedly had in mind our talmudic passage, which says that Abraham observed all the commandments, even the laws of festival preparation. It was by being *prepared* to observe all the commandments that Abraham in effect fulfilled them.

We now see that on one level the Hasidic homilists are entirely unoriginal. Every element they are to combine has already been established, and even a combination very like their own has already taken place. Our study has shown that, at least in our case, Scholem is quite right when he says that Hasidism is almost entirely unproductive of original ideas.[101] But even with the literary sources so clearly established, two essential questions still remain for the historian of Judaism: Why did these formulations, available long before the Hasidic movement, achieve such prominence in the circle of the Maggid's followers in the late eighteenth century, and how did Hasidism seek to respond to the challenge they raised? I have suggested an answer to the first of these by referring to Hasidism as a radical spiritualist movement in the context of post-rabbinic Judaism. The values of tradition and those of spiritual religion stand in tension with one another as the Maggid and his followers declare the realm of spirit to be the only reality and attachment to God to be the supreme religious value. It is in the course of needing to express such a claim in the language of Judaism that the Hasidic authors almost inevitably light upon Abraham, the spiritual seeker who did all out of love, fulfilling God's wishes—in whatever sense that is to be understood—even before they were commanded. If the Hasidic master seems, in the course of this search, to express a view that is closer to that of Philo or even Paul than it is to that of the talmudic rabbis, it is to a change in the structure of his situation, rather than to any historical influence, that this coincidence of views is due. To be sure, Paul's Abraham, who has faith before the Law, and the Hasidic Abraham, who fulfills the commandments in the spirit rather than in the flesh, do have something in common. Both Christianity and Hasidism in their earliest stages represent radical spiritualist movements emerging against the background of biblical Judaism. In different ways, each is struggling with the questions of law and obligation, piety and personal devotion. No wonder that both find in Abraham a figure who can represent a life of piety lived other than through devotion to details of law. For Paul's Christians, of course, this life outside the commandments represents a pattern to be followed. For the *Hasidim*—and, as we have shown, for Maimonides and others long before them—Abraham's faith serves as an inspiring example to strengthen them in their own piety, which is to be expressed through the commandments. If there is within the post-talmudic Jewish devotee a longing to follow the path of Abraham and worship God outside the Law, that desire is kept quite well hidden.

But it is now to the second and greater of these questions to which we must turn our attention. Once the tension between devotion and commandment came to the surface in Hasidism, that highly traditionalist form of popular mysticism, what did the leading thinkers of the movement do to prevent that perceived tension from creating a breach in practice as well?

V

We have seen that the radical spiritualist vision of early Hasidism created a certain tension between the values of the new movement and those of rabbinic Judaism in its classical forms. In choosing to express this tension by focusing on Abraham's "spiritual" fulfillment of the commandments, the Hasidic authors found a rubric from within the tradition itself which allowed them a degree of personal expression. Here as elsewhere, even their potentially "heretical" views were expressed in terms that were themselves tradition-affirming. In these discussions, we are able to catch a glimpse of the Hasidic master seeking to justify his own striving for a "higher" Judaism than that of devotion to the Law alone. But we should also note that the use of this aggadic theme was a relatively moderate way of making such a claim, one that befitted the movement's inner conservative tendency. The Kabbalistic tradition contained much stronger ways of expressing the dichotomy between law and spirit. Had the Hasidic masters truly sought to put themselves forth as rebels, they needed only to have referred to such existing notions as the claim that the commandments had existed in a purely spiritual state in Eden and that only due to the Fall had they taken on a corporeal form, or the idea that only at a particular point in cosmic history, coinciding with the second of the great Sabbatical cycles, did the eternal Torah become a document of law.[102] Both of these ideas, which were often conflated with one another, anticipate a time when law itself will be transcended and the Torah restored to its original "higher" state as a text of pure mystical speculation. They were to be found in books that were known to the Hasidic masters and that were even printed by the same printing houses that published the Hasidic works themselves. The total absence of these more radical ideas from the Hasidic sources is undoubtedly due to the fact that they had become "tainted" by their wide use in the theology of Sabbatianism. Reference to Abraham's devotion to *mizvot* in a spiritual fashion was a relatively conservative way of speaking about this inner tension. Surely it was safer to point to the pious Abraham who did all out of pure love and devotion than to articulate an attempt to return to the Edenic state before the Torah had become "sullied" by having to don the garments of this world.

The questions raised in Hasidism by the conflict of values between the radical spiritualistic ideal and commitment to the life of the commandments demanded an answer. In the time-honored fashion of traditional homilists, the disciples of Dov Baer of Miedzyrzec sought to guide their followers out of this dilemma. Abraham may have served by devotion alone, but we, living after Sinai, are given the *opportunity*, we have heard Levi Yizhak say, to worship in a more complete way, observing the *mizvot* even outside the Land of Israel. Sometimes the need for the regimen of law is seen as a negative comment on our spiritual state: only such giants as the patriarchs could follow the ways of God without the full complement of laws and statutes. More often, however, the service of Israel is contrasted with that of the angels; we who are created of flesh and blood as well as spirit are given the privilege of "turning darkness into light," something that is only possible because of our corporeal nature and the this-worldly way of service we have been granted. Still other passages defend the need for concrete actions as a part of worship on psychological grounds: the spirit or power aroused by the intensity of *kavvanah* requires a "vessel" to contain and thus sustain it. This explanation is, it should be noted, not alien to the spirit of more contemporary explanations of ritual among historians of religion.[103] These answers are provided in the same sporadic and occasional manner that characterizes the entire literature of early Hasidic preaching. When the question was raised, an answer was provided for it. Often as not, the answer was as much shaped by the need to fit it into an appropriate homiletic context as it was by the nature of the question as it was formulated.

In order to see a somewhat more systematic approach to our question, we must turn now to the schools of Bratslav and ḤaBaD. Here we address ourselves to the two most clearly articulated "systems" of thought to emerge within the world of early Hasidism. I use the word "system" somewhat guardedly, as none of the Hasidic masters produced what could be called a systematic theology in the Western sense of that term. In both cases we are essentially still dealing with homiletic works and short occasional pieces, though in the case of ḤaBaD there is also a single ordered treatise, *Liqquṭey Amarim* or *Tanya*. They are systems only in the sense of a general consistency of terminology and method extending over several works.[104] Bratslav Hasidism is essentially the creation of two men, Nahman ben Simhah of Bratslav (1772–1810), great-grandson of the Ba'al Shem Tov, and his chief disciple Nathan Sternharz (1780–1845) of Nemirov. The commandments are discussed only occasionally in Nahman's teachings, but Nathan's *Liqquṭey Halakhot* is a multi-volumed attempt to apply his master's thought to the laws of the *Shulḥan 'Arukh*, the authoritative code of Jewish practice. ḤaBaD theology is primarily the creation of four thinkers, three of them members of the same family and leaders of the ḤaBaD/Lubavich community. The founder of the ḤaBaD system was Shne'ur Zalman of Liadi (1745–1813), called the "elder rabbi" by the Lubavich *hasidim*. His two leading disciples were his own son, Dov Baer of Lubavich (1773–1827), the "middle rabbi," and Aaron Ha-Levi Horowitz of Starroselje

(1766–1828). A grandson of Shne'ur Zalman, Menahem Mendal Schneersohn (1789–1866), became the third master of Lubavich; his work *Derekh Mizvotekha* is the major source for ḤaBaD treatment of the commandments.

Students of Hasidism, including myself, have generally presented ḤaBaD and Bratslav as two *opposing* schools within Hasidic thought; the late Joseph Weiss contrasted them as "The Hasidism of Mysticism and the Hasidism of Faith."[105] It would behoove us here, however, before discussing their respective treatments of the commandments, to note a number of features that these two schools have in common.

The origins of both Bratslav and ḤaBaD represent Hasidism in its heyday, just before and after the turn of the nineteenth century. Shne'ur Zalman became the leader of Byelorussian Hasidism in the 1780s, following the emigration of Menahem Mendel of Vitebsk to the Holy Land in 1777. His best-known work, the *Tanya* (properly titled *Liqqutey Amarim*), was published in 1796. Nahman's ministry began upon his return from a mysterious journey to *Erez Yisra'el* in 1799 and intensified with his move to Bratslav in 1802. Both Nahman and Shne'ur Zalman saw themselves as beleaguered by enemies, Nahman's coming from within the Hasidic camp and Shne'ur Zalman's primarily from without. Both systems were developed partially in response to real or assumed criticism. The creative periods of both schools reached well into the middle of the nineteenth century, when their respective works on the commandments were composed.[106]

On a more inward level, it may be said that both Bratslav and ḤaBaD represent partial disaffection with the Hasidism of the BeSHT and the Maggid, and in each case there is a return, though of a rather different sort, to the pre-Hasidic Kabbalah. Nahman of Bratslav, beset by states of depression and feelings of alienation from God, was ill-served by the enthusiastic pantheism that lay at the core of his great-grandfather's teachings. As I have shown elsewhere, Nahman sought to encompass his own doubts within a dialectical notion of faith; divine transcendence and the reality of *zimzum*, God's withdrawal from the world, are essential categories of his thought, in an attempt to account for the absence of God from ordinary human experience. An overpowering sense of guilt creates in him a strong attraction to asceticism, recreating for Bratslav Hasidism some of the *ethos* of pre-Hasidic Kabbalah in Eastern Europe. The sense of divine immediacy in the religion of the BeSHT and the relief it provided from the burden of sin are lost in Bratslav. Shne'ur Zalman of Liadi, a talmudic scholar of repute before he joined the Maggid's circle, was frightened by the implications of the radical acosmicism that he saw in his own Hasidic teachings as well as in those of others. In addition to re-asserting the primacy of Torah study as the way of divine service, which we shall see presently, he also returned to a use of Kabbalistic language and thought patterns which had been largely set aside by his Hasidic contemporaries. He did so out of a need to reconstitute the carefully annotated psychic map which the Kabbalists had once possessed, but which had been swept aside by the wave of Hasidic enthusiasm.[107] It was precisely for this that he was criticized by his fellow Miedzyrzec disciple Abraham of Kalisk, who accused him of confusing the minds of ordinary folk by "garbing the teachings of the BeSHT in the teachings of Luria."[108]

In both of these grand edifices of Hasidic thought, the need for subjugation of the self to the divine *will* also takes on a larger role than it had in previous Hasidic discourse. Both Nahman and Shne'ur Zalman view the service of God as involving an ongoing struggle to submit human will to the divine command, an issue that does not seem to have much troubled such thinkers as Levi Yizhak of Berdichev or Menahem Nahum of Chernobyl. Nahman is constantly and painfully aware that the battle is ever on the brink of being lost; the outcry and demand for broken-hearted contrition that fill his writings are largely the result of this sense of near-failure to control the will. Shne'ur Zalman's vision is more the balanced attempt to achieve something of the Maimonidean golden mean in the Hasidic context. The *benoni* who is the object of the *Tanya's* intention is a person who has wholly subjected his own still-felt passions to the demands of God's will as expressed in the halakhic system. Even though Shne'ur Zalman is not fascinated by the struggle itself, as Nahman is, this subjugation of self is clearly no small task, to hear the *Tanya* tell of it.

VI

There are rather few teachings in Nahman's *Liqqutey MoHaRaN* that deal directly either with the commandments as a whole or with reasons for specific *mizvot*. Nahman seems to be more concerned with issues of faith and obstacles to it than he is with specific matters of observance, which were still largely taken for granted in his world. If there were a few Jews who were becoming lax in their religious practice, some of whom he encountered toward the end of his life, he was convinced that it was the general intellectual issues of faith and doubt that had led them astray, and it was on these that he focused his attention.

The constant struggle for faith that characterizes Nahman's religious life is clearly one that has no room for full intellectual comprehension of the commandments. Nahman's position is on the one hand that of a simple fideist who lives the life of Torah because God has commanded it, and on the other that of a mystic who strives to reach such a state of oneness with God that the divine will becomes entirely his own. It is Nahman the fideist who says

> It was out of God's love for Israel and His desire that they cleave to Him and love Him by means of this corporeal world that He cloaked His divinity in the measured forms [*middot*] of Torah. These are the 613 commandments: God measured out in His mind that by means of this specific commandment we would be able to attain to Him, and that is why He contracted His divinity into these 613 precise commandments. He determined in His mind, for example, the commandment of *tefillin*, deciding that it would have to be precisely this way with four portions of text contained in four compartments and straps of leather . . . It was in this particular way we could reach Him, and that is why He did not ordain compartments of gold or silver.[109]

Each detail of the commandments is given by God in the precise manner that will allow, for reasons we cannot understand, for our maximal attainment of closeness to Him, the goal of Nahman's Hasidic piety. But Nahman also knows that such attainment is not so simple. Each Jew, he said, lives ever with the phrase *na'aseh ve-nishma‛*—"We shall do and we shall listen"—on his lips: "We shall do" refers to the level at which we comprehend and act upon Torah; "we shall listen" indicates that there are always levels of mystery accompanying the deed that we have not yet fathomed, that which we still need to "hear." He goes on to say that

> On each and every rung, in each and every world, there exist "we shall do" and "we shall listen." Each according to his level has a "we shall do," that is, Torah as it is revealed to him, and a "we shall listen," hidden things, [identified with] prayer. As a person moves up to a higher rung, his "we shall listen" becomes a "we shall do," and he gets another "we shall listen." Thus it goes from rung to rung.[110]

This helix of ascent leads ultimately entirely beyond the self into a mystical identification with the Torah and even the prayer of God.

> One must ever go from rung to rung, higher and higher, until one reaches the first point of Creation, the beginning of divine emanation [*keter*, the will of God, or its first manifestation in *hokhmah*]. There too one finds "we shall do" and "we shall hear."
> The "hearing" which is found there is the true Torah of God. . . . There is a Torah of God Himself, to which our sages refer as follows: "I was the first to fulfill it"; "The Blessed Holy One clothes the naked, visits the sick," etc.; "How do we know that the Blessed Holy One puts on *tefillin*?" etc.[111]

While there is a kind of "understanding" that has importance in each stage of this process, it does not seem to be of a truly intellectual kind, but rather a constant strengthening of one's inner resistance to doubt. The one who reaches the final rung of mystical identification fulfills the commandments as God fulfills them, not because of any intellectual understanding he has achieved, but because he has reached a point where the process of understanding itself is dwarfed by the mystic's identification with the divine reality. Meanwhile, for those who have not attained that ultimate state, there are only the struggle and the demand to stretch ever upward. This sense of the need for constant spiritual growth and ascent lay at the very core of Nahman's religious life, to which complacency and self-satisfaction were depicted as the greatest enemies.

There is a single but most important reference in Nahman's published teachings to the question of Torah before Sinai. In the very last teaching he offered before his tragic and untimely death,[112] Nahman was especially revealing about his own inner religious conflicts. He spoke of times when he felt unable to teach or to offer anything at all to his disciples; at such moments the way of Torah became closed to him. These were times when he "knew nothing at all" and was like an entirely ordinary person. But if we believe that life itself derives from Torah, the dying Nahman went on to say, how can I—he refers, as usual in such passages, to "the *zaddiq*"—be sustained even for a moment outside it? At such times, he suggests, he is sustained by *derekh erez*, "the way of the world," which, according to the Rabbis, preceded Torah.[113] *Derekh erez* has many meanings in Jewish sources, but in Nahman's mouth here it refers to the simplicity of life in patriarchal times, a period "when the world was sustained by *hesed* alone." He refers, of course, to the religious life of Abraham, as described in the Kabbalistic sources we have quoted earlier. Nahman is able to return to those times in such moments of extreme "ordinariness," when the diet of Torah, if you will, is too rich to sustain him. At such times his extraordinarily fertile but also tortured mind does not produce its usual feats of creative mental gymnastics in the reinterpretation of Torah. We cannot but wonder whether it was only the ability to create original teachings that eluded him in such moments, or whether the *life* of Torah and commandments itself might have been beyond his power when he faced his deeper depressions.[114] In any case, we are made aware by this passage that for Nahman the world of pre-Sinaitic existence is not only a dim memory of ancient times, but is one that remains somehow spiritually accessible in the present.

Most of the Bratslav material concerning the commandments is found in the writings of Nathan of Nemirov. His *Liqqutey Hal-akhot* takes the form of a multi-volume commentary to the *Shulhan 'Arukh*. Actually it is a continuation of Nahman's *oeuvre*, each section beginning with the application of one of Nahman's teachings to a paragraph of the Law and then going on with the disciple's own lengthy (and frequently repetitive) commentary. While Nathan applies Hasidic thought here to a halakhic text, the work could hardly be called halakhic in nature. Most of it is filled with extended aggadic homily, punctuated with frequent attempts to explain the codified precept, including details of its observance not listed in the code itself, in accord with Nahman's teachings. Underlying this treatment is the disciple's firm belief that his master's teachings are the unique key to unlocking the mysteries contained within the Law. Nathan, who lived into the fifth decade of the nineteenth century, saw much more than his master had of the spread of enlightenment or, from his point of view, of apostasy and heresy. This may have been what motivated him to apply his master's method to the code of religious praxis. In general he is much more conservative and pietistic than was his rather daring master.

Nathan's opening comment on the laws of reciting the *shema'* offers a brief illustration of his method. Here we find a clear and rather concise example of his Hasidic defense of *halakhah*, intended to show how the details of proper observance as codified in the Law point to mysteries discussed in Nahman's teachings. He opens by referring to a statement his master had made regarding prayer, in which he said how hard it was, if one had full concentration in prayer, to move on from one word to the next. Only by making the entire prayer-service into one (we think here of a reversal of Nahmanides' reading of Torah as a single word!) can you reach the end of the service without having yet "abandoned" even the first letter. This can be done, Nahman goes on to say, only by *biṭṭul el ha-takhlit*, "negation [of the self] before the Ultimate," which is his way of describing the mystical moment. Here Nathan picks up the thread:

> Reciting the *shema'* is negating oneself before the Ultimate, as it says "The Lord our God, the Lord is One." That means that "on that day the Lord shall be one and His name one" (Zech. 14:9), as RaSHI explains it.[115] This is "the all-good" and "The Lord, He is God" (I Kings 8:60).[116] Of this Scripture says: "I praise the word in the Lord; I praise the word in God" (Ps. 56:11). This is "the Lord our God, the

Lord is One"—all one and all good. This is the meaning of "Hear,
O Israel"—"Cause your ear to hear what your mouth is saying,"[117]
as the Rabbis explained. But this would lead you to remain with the
first letter, and the only way out of this is to look to the Ultimate—"the
Lord our God, the Lord is One."

Only concentration on "the Ultimate" or on the absolute unity
of God can save one from fragmentation in prayer, from becoming so attached to the beauty of a single word or letter that one
cannot move onward. The very fulfillment of "Hear, O Israel"
could itself lead one astray. The only help is in total devotion to
God's oneness, in which the very distinction between one word
and the next loses its meaning. This oneness is depicted by the
unification of the names *YHWH* and *Elohim*, ("Lord" and "God"
in our translation), the two chief biblical locutions for the deity.
Their union in the mystic's mind presages the final moment of
which the prophet speaks, the time in which all will be declared
"good" and no further distinction will need be made between the
blessing at hearing good tidings and that for accepting ill fate.

That is why the Rabbis were also able to derive from this verse that
shema' may be recited in any language, saying that "Hear" means
"in any language that you comprehend." Once you have negated
yourself before the Ultimate, where all is one and all is good, there
is no evil present at all. The evil of the [heathen] languages falls
away and is negated; only the good that had been robed within that
language remains.[118] For surely all the languages contain hidden
goodness, but the evil hides it. That is why it is improper to recite
statutory public prayers [Heb.: *davar shebi-qedushah*] in other languages.
But the *shema'*, which itself implies a negation before the all-good,
can be said in any language. That is why the evidence that there is
good in all languages is found right in the *shema'*, as the rabbis said
about "they shall be *totafot* between your eyes," explaining this word
as derived from *tat* which means "two" in "Coptic" and *fat* which
means "two" in "African" [referring to the four parchment chambers
in the *head-tefillin*].[119] Here the goodness of the holy tongue is dressed
in the languages of the nations, just as our master taught. . . .

Now we also understand a law about which the decisors have
raised some question. Why did our Rabbis interpret "When you lie
down and when you rise up" in such a way that the former phrase

permits the *shema*'s recitation at any time during the night, "As long as it is lying-down time," while the latter phrase is taken to refer to the time of rising, the beginning of the day but not the entire day.[120] [The answer is that] the essential recital of the *shema*', which is the negation [of self], is only at night. This is the closing of the eyes, the time when people rest from their this-worldly pursuits. Our master has said elsewhere[121] that this negation takes place chiefly at night. Night is also the time of stern judgments, the suffering that leads one to negation,[122] as our master says there. This is the meaning of "When I dwell in darkness the Lord is my light"; this is the light that is greater [when contrasted with] the dark. At the time when darkness, judgments, and suffering overwhelm one, whether in matters of worship or in worldly matters, the best advice is to close one's eyes and negate oneself before the Ultimate, that which is all-good. Then all the suffering will itself be negated. This is sleep, which belongs to the night. In sleep we transcend ourselves, saying "In Your hands I place my spirit". . . .[123] That is why we recite the *shema*' at bedtime . . . so the main recital of *shema*' is at night, and its time is all the night, the time of [self-]negation.

Day is not really the time of *shema*' recital, except for the time when we first get up, before people have begun to spread forth in pursuit of worldly goals. This [beginning of the day] is still a time of shut eyes, but afterwards the *shema*' can no longer be recited. That is why the Rabbis fixed the time limit for reciting the [morning] *shema*' to the latest point when some people in the world are still asleep, "the hour when princes arise from their beds." Only before all have arisen is the world still [somewhat] at rest, but after the third hour [of the day] when everyone is awake, it is no longer time for the *shema*'.[124]

The opening discussion of the Mishnah has here been given a framework of meaning that derives in a direct sense from Nahman's teachings. The Bratslav *hasid*, who is the intended reader of this text, has the daily praxis justified for him in terms of his master's teachings. In fact the reverse is also true: the truth value of Nahman's teachings is enhanced by Nathan's demonstration of how well they fit the universally accepted details of the Law. The fact is, furthermore, that all of the elements used in these explications long antedate Nahman of Bratslav. The non-Bratslav reader would find little here with which to quarrel. The associations of night, fear, mortal danger, and suffering (including the suffering of exile) are an ancient aggadic motif, a theme that finds strong reflection in the text of the prayerbook itself. The *shemaʿ* as the proclamation of God's unity before which all else is negated has a long history in Jewish mysticism, and Nathan's views certainly would not have been contradicted within Hasidic circles. Nahman's own contribution to all this lies in the pattern of near-free association that ties diverse elements together in unique ways;[125] indeed, it is on these associations that the *novellae* of Nathan's work are often based. But the combination of legal, biblical, and Kabbalistic elements is so thorough in Nathan's writings that one would sometimes be hard put to isolate exactly what about his justification of the commandments is specific to Bratslav teaching. The struggle for faith and the battle against despair are here fully integrated into the ongoing daily way of life that constitutes traditional Judaism. In this example, the purpose of the law (the obligation to recite the *shemaʿ*) is to lead us to self-transcendence; the details surrounding that law (its recitation at any time during the night) remind us of how that transcendence can be best effectuated.

In thinking about this reading of the commandments in the context of earlier mystical *taʿamey ha-mizvot*, we want to note that the "secret" revealed by the commandments here is quite different from that sought by the earlier Kabbalists. The reference here is to an attainable human state, that of self-negation. In other Bratslav passages, it is to a moral goal or a new rung in the constantly ongoing struggle for self-perfection. The *hasid* is not interested in the sefirotic secrets of the *mizvot* for their own sake. References to the "upper worlds" will occur in Nathan's explanations only when he can bring them also "down to earth" as a moralist.[126] The *hasid* speaks a language related to that of the Kabbalistic ethical treatises, except that *here the self, rather than the cosmos, stands as the object of his purifying efforts.* Kabbalah insisted, against the philosophic tradition, that the *mizvot* were the fulfillment of divine need [*zorekh gavoha*], and that the cosmos was to be restored through their performance. This tradition is still to be found in early Hasidism, though it is often transferred to the realm of "worship through corporeal things," the seeing of all of human life as an act of worship for the sake of God. In Bratslav it is primarily the redemption of the individual that is at stake. In a spiritual world in which sin is overpoweringly real and from which God is distant because of human sin, the essential purpose of the commandments is (paradoxically, from Paul's point of view!) to lighten the burden by bringing about a gradual uplifting and transformation of the fallen human spirit. Daily recitation of the *shema'* can bring us one step closer, at least in our minds, to the ultimate state in which the breach between good and ill will be repaired and the unity of God will encompass all of being.

VII

The intellectual/spiritual world of ḤaBaD is in this way quite far from that of Bratslav. Nahman's preoccupation with human sinfulness was not shared by Shne'ur Zalman, who in general was more devoted to the mystical "high road" of leading the self to an encounter with the divine reality, trusting that this would transform the moral character as well, rather than the "low road" of worrying first about moral self-perfection as preparation for the encounter with God.[127]

Shne'ur Zalman accepts from his teacher the Maggid the awareness that all of material existence is but a veiling of the divine reality. The acosmic theology of the Miedzyrzec school in fact achieves its clearest and most unequivocal expression in the second section of Shne'ur Zalman's *Tanya*, a work intended for popular consumption. He is absolutely thoroughgoing there in his insistence that from the divine point of view there exists no world at all; Deuteronomy 4:39 is taken to mean: "Know this day and set it upon your heart that the divine source of life and the hiding of that source are One, and there exists nothing else!" In his theological essays,[128] Shne'ur Zalman goes even further than others in the Maggid's school, insisting that the light of *Eyn Sof*—a Cordoveran Kabbalistic term of which he is particularly fond—exists everywhere in absolute equality. There is no difference between "upper" and "lower" worlds except in the degree to which the light is hidden or revealed to us: metaphysically all distinctions are but illusion. Much of Shne'ur Zalman's theological *oeuvre* is dedicated to the obliteration of any distinction between transcendence and immanence. The transcendent God and the immanent God—called *sovev* and *memale'*, respectively, in ḤaBaD nomenclature—are seen as distinct from one another only due to the inadequacy of human understanding, an inadequacy that the mystical training of ḤaBaD is designed to help one overcome.[129]

Because of this refinement in the Maggid's theological position, the earlier Hasidic view of the "uplifting" of sparks as the central focus of the devotional life did not fit well into Shne'ur Zalman's theology. While this familiar theme is by no means entirely absent from his work, the motifs of "hiding" and "revealing" now take a more central role than those of "descent" and "ascent." The existence of this world, such as it is, represents a voluntary self-hiding by God; the progress of the mystic in attaining spiritual awareness is the bringing of God into a revealed state. Here we perforce encounter one of several paradoxes that characterize the language of ḤaBaD mysticism: if the goal of mystical religious life is the undoing of that which God has chosen to do, is not the mystic path a contravention of God's will? By what right does the mystic so train his mind as to bring into the light of day that which the Holy One has chosen to make hidden? The fact is, Shne'ur Zalman would claim, that God desires the revealing as well as the hiding. The *ultimate* divine purpose is that it be known that God is everywhere One, that *sovev* and *memale'* are indistinct from one another, and—again paradoxically—that there exists a human society that lives in cognizance of this reality. But the ordinary human mind cannot handle the truth that God (encompassing all of being) is One. The human self is needed (here the influence of the Maggid reasserts itself) to transform darkness into light, to show that divinity can be found even in the corporeal realm. The reason our consciousness cannot naturally bear the awareness that all is God is our attachment to the body, to the corporeal state. And this attachment is no mere accident or spiritual detriment, but is of the very essence of our task. God wants us to be worldly, attached to the material plane, so that we can mystically transform it into divine Nothingness, just as much as He wants us to be aware of the fact that this material existence is illusory and the "transformation" is in fact no transformation at all, but only a realization of the truth.

These two prongs, if you will, of the divine intent for humanity call for two distinct forms of divine service. There is an *'avodah* which is designed to help the person overcome worldliness and to see that all is one in God; this is the service of prayer and especially of contemplation, a skill that is highly developed and much discussed, especially in the writings of ḤaBaD's second generation. But there is also a form of service that is intended specifically to *attach* the person to the material world, to increase his degree of involvement with corporeality so that he will be able to uplift it. This is the service of God through Torah and the commandments, which takes on a central theoretical as well as a practical role in the life of ḤaBaD Hasidism.[130]

Shne'ur Zalman, the Torah scholar and intellectualist mystic, seeks to turn the focus of Hasidism away from the emphasis on "worship through corporeal things" as it was defined by others in the Maggid's school. For Menahem Nahum of Chernobyl or Ephraim of Sudilkow, *'avodah be-gashmiyut* meant chiefly the service of God through ordinary acts of human living in addition to that by means of the specific commandments.[131] Not so for Shne'ur Zalman. All of human activity is to be seen as belonging to the sphere of "worship." God has given us the commandments, just as He has made us in bodily form, so that we may "transform" the world through them. It is the specific act of worship through the commandments that has this power, and it is deed rather than *kavvanah* that releases it.[132] Here Shne'ur Zalman is truly breaking with the values of Hasidism, which had insisted that deeds without inner direction of the heart were meaningless empty shells that could not "fly upward" to heaven. For ḤaBaD, the *performance* of the commandments, including the *miẓvah* of Torah study, is the only way to know God in this world. In a well-known parable, Shne'ur Zalman compares the *miẓvot* to a servant's embrace of the King through His royal garments. It is only because of this garb of the King that one has any chance of embracing Him at all. Though it is true that the servant is touching the clothing rather than the King Himself, the knowledge that the King is present inside these garments suffices for him as an experience of intimacy with the royal self.[133] Of course the other side of *'avodah*, namely, the realization that garments, servant, and even "King" are but illusion, is not far from the devotee's mind when he performs such an act of seemingly "simple" worship.

Following earlier precedents, Hasidism spoke of three realms within which God was to be worshipped: thought, speech, and action. In the usual Hasidic hierarchy of values, thought was the highest of these three realms and action was the lowest. *Maḥashavah* in fact represented the upper sefirotic universe for the Kabbalists, while *dibbur* represented *malkhut*, the intermediate realm between the divine and worldly. *Ma'aseh* in this schema would represent the lower world itself, the corporeal universe that could only be transformed by the relatively "coarse" character of physical actions.[134] Now Shne'ur Zalman stands this system on its head, claiming that action is the highest form of divine service through the commandments, because only the deed itself fulfills the divine will for corporealization through human agency. The person must actually enter into the corporeal realm by the performance of *mizvot* in order that corporeality itself ultimately be negated through the contemplative soul. For the will of God who wants us to make the physical real—at least temporarily so—only action can do. The historian of Judaism cannot help but note here the final stage in the transformation of the Sabbatian motif, still alive in early Hasidism, of "descent for the sake of ascent"—here the "descent" itself can be accomplished only by the performance of a *mizvah*!

As a specific example of the ḤaBaD treatment of a *mizvah*, I have chosen its understanding of a commandment to which the followers of Shne'ur Zalman have particularly sought to devote themselves over the generations, the *mizvah* of *ahavat yisra'el*, love for one's fellow Jew. The interpretation of this obligation as presented in Menaḥem Mendel Schneersohn's *Derekh Mizvotekha* will provide us a good "window" on the place of the commandments in ḤaBaD thought as a whole. Menaḥem Mendel's homiletic style

is a bit drawn out, and careful attention will be needed in following his line of argument.[135]

> The commandment of the love of Israel [contains two parts]: not to
> hate your fellow, as Scripture says: "You shall not hate your brother
> in your heart" (Lev. 19:17) and to love every person of Israel, as it
> says: "Love your neighbor as yourself" (ibid. 18). The statement of
> Hillel the Elder[136] to the convert is well known: "That which is
> hateful to you, do not to your fellow. This is the entire Torah; the
> rest is commentary." Hillel's words are not easily understood. We
> might accept them regarding the commandments between man and
> man, but how do they apply to the commandments between man
> and God? [Of these] Scripture further says: "If you are righteous,
> what do you give Him?" (Job 35:7). We also know that before
> [morning] prayers it is customary to declare: "I hereby accept upon
> myself the positive commandment "Love your neighbor as your-
> self,"[137] for this is fundamental to the service of God. But we need
> to understand this matter.

The author begins his disquisition by quoting sources that emphasize the importance of loving one's fellow Jew for worship or
for fulfilling one's obligations to God. He asks why it is that the
"vertical" relationship between God and the individual Jew should
be so deeply affected by the seemingly "horizontal" obligation to
love one's fellow.

> In the work *Ta'amey ha-Mizvot*, section *Qedoshim*, Rabbi Isaac Luria
> writes:[138] "All of Israel are the single body of the soul of Adam; each
> Israelite is a particular limb. From this derives the responsibility of
> each Jew for the other if he sins. That is why my teacher [Luria
> himself] had the custom of reciting each detail of the confessional
> [even confessing sins he himself had not committed], because all of
> Israel are a single body."
>   The meaning of his words is as follows: Adam contained within
> himself all the souls of Israel, except for those which will appear only
> after the resurrection. Some of these souls stemmed from his head,
> others from his arm, and so forth. That is why he is called Adam,
> because of the verse *eddammeh la-'elyon*, "I shall be like unto the most
> high" (Is. 14:14). He, the all-inclusive one, stemmed from that aspect
> of Adam above [the Adam Qadmon figure that preceded the *sefirot*,
> according to Lurianic teaching], which included all the ten *sefirot* as
> a configuration. Of this Scripture says: "My first-born son, Israel"

(Ex. 4:22). . . . In this way we also understand that the souls of Israel together constitute a complete bodily form, which is the all-embracing soul of Adam.

The notion that all Jews share responsibility for one another is an ancient one, painfully reinforced by the experience of Jewish history. The Kabbalists carried this idea much further, seeing the entire community of Israel as a single body. They attached this vision to the myth of Adam Qadmon, a primal emanation of divinity that contained the entire cosmos. The human Adam was an earthly embodiment of Adam Qadmon, and he contained within him all the souls of Israel. The question of non-Jewish souls—obviously also descended from Adam—and their place in this scheme is ignored by the Kabbalist.

Even though [the soul] contains 248 distinguishable limbs, all of them are included within one another. This can be understood in the case of an individual person; even though one's limbs are distinct from one another, head, feet, nails, and so forth, nevertheless each one of these contains them all. There is in the hand something of the life-flow of the foot, through the veins that course through it. The same is true of all the other limbs, and one limb is healed, as we know, by the letting of blood in another [!], because the blood is mixed. This mutual inclusion of the limbs and the life within them is due to the fact that they are all included in that single flow of life that shines into the brain. Only afterwards are they separated into specific limbs, but the brain embraces them all, just like *hyle* [includes all material things that were derived from it]. Thus it is the brain that is sensitive to all the limbs, feeling the pain in a hand or a foot, in the same way. Sometimes, in fact, the brain feels greater pain because of a blow on the fingernail than it does from a blow on the hand itself, as we know from experience.

It is in this sense that the 248 limbs of Adam are joined to one another. It is because the source of his soul was in the upper *hokhmah* of Adam above, the aspect of *Eyn Sof* that dwells in unity with its Wisdom, for "He and His wisdom are One"[139]. . . . but after the soul of Adam was divided into multiple roots, and each of these into multiple branches and sparks in the particular bodies, the situation is like that of the body's divided limbs. The hand does not feel pain in the foot, which is separated from it, and so forth. But this separation is only from the body's point of view; on the level of soul there is in fact no separation and all of them fit together, just as the hand contains those same veins that reach into the foot and the eye, and so forth. In spirit it has, therefore, tremendous pain from the hurt of the eye, as we have expressed it in the parable. That is why Luria recited every detail of the confessional, for the sin that any Jew might have committed. He was like the parent of that limb in which that Jew's soul was rooted; the pain reached the higher limb (i.e., the head) where Luria's soul was rooted. . . .

That is also why we are commanded to love every Jew: everyone is made up of all the souls of Israel, as is the case with the limbs. Thus the other is also within you, and you thus must love the other as yourself. You too are similarly included within the other in this linkage of limbs. This is why it is necessary to accept this *mizvah* before praying, for when you offer up your soul in the word "One" (of the *shema'*) . . . this ascent cannot be whole or fit unless it contains all souls within it. . . .[140]

Menahem Mendel has spelled out the "mystical biology" of the unity of souls in some detail. All the souls of Israel are not only bound together in origin, but contain elements of one another. It is only the spiritual blindness of our illusory isolation into individual psyches that prevents our seeing this reality. The unity of all Jewish souls as one is a part, of course, of the greater vision of cosmic unity that underlies all of ḤaBaD thought.[141] But in good Kabbalistic fashion, each such partial unity in itself expresses an important part of the truth. ḤaBaD, as a systematic, step-by-step educational plan for the cultivation of mystical awareness, is not interested merely in sweeping statements about the unity of all being, but seeks rather to inculcate that value at each and every turn. It is the awareness of the *zaddiq*, here exemplified by Luria, that all separation between Jewish souls is illusory, which our author would like to inculcate in his readers. But this reality, if it is not to degenerate into platitudes, needs concrete expression in the interpersonal sphere:

Now this inclusion really takes place only when a person demonstrates with his very self and body that he loves his neighbor, like two limbs joined to one another, fulfilling "What's mine is yours,"[142] for the other is his own flesh and blood. This cannot happen when you hate anyone of Israel in your heart; then you separate the portion of that person from your soul, pushing him away in hatred. You remove your will from him, and thus you of necessity have a blemish or a lack in your own soul, a place where that portion is missing . . . and you remain blemished . . . then you cannot rise up in an acceptable way before God, as Scripture says: "The one that has a blemish may not draw near to be offered up" (Lev. 21:17). The light of *Eyn Sof* which contains them all will not bear you, because of the lack in you, since you have left that one out. *Eyn Sof*, after all, contains him as well. . . .

[This is the meaning of] "Bless us, our Father, all of us as One."[143] For then "You are all beautiful, my beloved, and there is no blemish in you" (Cant. 4:7). Then the union of the Blessed Holy One and His *shekhinah* is effected, revealing the light of *Eyn Sof* in the source of Israel's souls, "so that they be One within One. . . ."[144] This is the secret meaning of "You shall be perfect with the Lord your God" (Deut. 18: 13). Just as God is perfect [simple, whole] with the totality of Israel's souls, shining the light of sublime *hokhmah* into these limbs of the *shekhinah*, loving His neighbor as Himself and disregarding his sins, so must you be whole and simple with your neighbors, so that the Lord may be your God in complete devotion, in Oneness.

This is why Hillel said: "The rest is commentary": all the *mizvot* are for the purpose of uniting the Holy One and His *shekhinah*, as is known. . . . This union is dependent upon the revealing of true love, so that the other be truly "as yourself," for "His people are a part of God" (Deut. 32:9), as we have explained. And this comes about through the fulfillment of "Love your neighbor as yourself," to which all the other commandments are thus a commentary, spelling out this union.

The cultivation of awareness that all souls are one, including the realization of such awareness in the realm of human action, brings about unity within God as well, based on the Kabbalistic understanding that the performance of *mizvot* in this world affects the divine cosmos. The oneness and perfection of God is reasserted by our affirmation in deed of our oneness with each person of Israel. As such, the *mizvah* of loving Jews is no different from that of donning *tefillin* or waving the *lulav*. But here the parallel between the sefirotic unity above and the human unity below lends an added measure of poetic and moral reality to the claim.

I have translated this teaching on the commandment of *ahavat yisra'el* at some length, not only because of its inherent beauty or value, but because it illustrates how Hasidism has come full circle with regard to the question of spirituality and the commandments.

Menahem Mendel of Lubavitch was *rebbe* until 1866. He was a major opponent, on both the intellectual and political battlefields, of the mid-century Russian *haskalah*.[145] Here Hasidism has fully entered into the role of champion of orthodoxy, defending the *mizvot* against a real and active threat. At the same time, Lubavich was a tradition in which the radically spiritualist and acosmic position was very much alive; *Tanya* was studied and memorized by every ḤaBaDnik and formed the basis of all later ḤaBaD literature. Menahem Mendel here uses the spiritualist argument to defend the *mizvah*. The reason you must love your fellow Jew and must reconfirm your love for him each morning is that you and he (along with the rest of reality, though he does not say so here) are really one in God. That sense of being one with the source, potentially a reason for feeling the inadequacy of this-worldly commandments, *is here a basis of the commandments themselves.* The commandments exist for the sake of the unification of God. Israel, the unifier—here in the Kabbalistic sense—must itself be one before it can embark on this sacred task.

The love of fellow Jew is a commandment that hovers between the realms of the abstract and the concrete. Though seemingly a matter for the heart alone, Menahem Mendel makes it clear that this love needs to be made manifest in concrete action, including self-sacrifice. It is only by this concretization in deed of the commandment to love that the devotee dares to show himself before God in prayer, which is the retransformation of that reality into abstraction.

The tension in ḤaBaD thought between the twin divine imperatives of concretization and abstraction or self-annihilation of which we have spoken goes right to the heart of that which motivates the entire theological *oeuvre* of the ḤaBaD school. The two divine wills represent a projection onto God of the twin wills of ḤaBaD's founder and leaders, the desire to be one with God, to know that all is illusion and to experience its nullification, and at the same time to remain faithful to the life of study, observance, and conventional piety as they were carried out in the world that gave birth to this mystical system. Here we indeed see how deeply the conventionally pious mystic is filled with ambivalence. He has seen through to the root of being, to the Oneness of all existence. In the world of this vision there is seemingly no place for the small-minded concerns of halakhic detail. Even the study of Torah, concentrated on talmudic dialectics, is hard to imagine when nought but God exists. And yet the *halakhah* must be preserved; the mystic's loyalty to traditional Judaism as the source from which all his spiritual nourishment has been attained cannot be compromised. Nothing short of the use of mystical teaching itself to defend the commandments can save the day, and mysticism must be stood on its head, if need be, to do so.

It might also be helpful to see this polarity of concretization and annihilation within ḤaBaD thought as representing two streams within religion, both of them widely found in the sources of mysticism. We refer to the dichotomy between the spiritualistic and the sacramental.[146] The former strives tirelessly for the realization of spirit in all things or the knowledge that all is God, always aiming for more pure and total spiritualization of self, world, and teaching. The latter contents itself with effecting divine presence *within* this world by the creation of certain powerful *symbols* of transformation; making the divine incarnate or tangible through specific forms is its goal. Both of these religious categories are part of the legacy of Hasidism. The original tendency of the movement was toward the spiritualistic; this was the core experience of the Ba'al Shem Tov, so it would seem, and it was also a message appropriate to the radical awakening Hasidism felt was needed by Jewry in the mid-eighteenth century. We have seen how far this spiritualistic vision went in the Hasidic treatments of Abraham and the commandments. Though the *mizvot* in practice do not seem to have been threatened, the longing for a "higher" or more wholly spiritual religion was a strong one. The masters of ḤaBaD, feeling this tendency to have gone too far, turned back to the old Kabbalistic sacramental vision as an antidote. The theurgic power attached to the actual performance of *mizvot*, rooted in the identification between the commandments and the sefirotic world, was now reintroduced into Hasidism by that school which was accused of "garbing the teachings of the BeSHT in the teachings of Luria."[147]

Indeed it was in the pre-Hasidic Kabbalah, itself created in the thirteenth century in response to an earlier perceived threat to the life of the commandments, that ḤaBaD found a rich realm of associative links between the mysteries of the upper worlds and the deeper meanings of the *mizvot*. It was to that realm which these mystics, who knew full well on another level that all but God was utter illusion, now turned, in order to seek out such profound teachings as would transform, and thus mystically redeem, the commandments themselves.

Notes

1. This dual character of institutional religion, and especially of ritual, has generally been overlooked in the recent scientific literature. It has been treated briefly by Martin Buber in his essay "Symbolic and Sacramental Existence," in *The Origin and Meaning of Hasidism* (New York: Harper and Row, 1960), p. 166ff. This essay is undoubtedly influenced by the categories of Friedrich Nietzsche's *The Birth of Tragedy*, as is the rather parallel discussion of language in H. N. Bialik's "Revealment and Concealment in Language," translated in R. Alter's *Modern Hebrew Literature* (New York: Behrman, 1975).

2. See Ephraim E. Urbach, "When Old Prophecy Ceased," *Tarbiz 17* (1946): I-II; id., "Halacha and Prophecy," *Tarbiz* 18 (1947): 1–27. On canon, see Joel Rosenberg, "Biblical Tradition: Literature and Spirit in Ancient Israel," in my *Jewish Spirituality I* (New York: Crossroad, 1986), pp. 82–89.

3. In *On the Kabbalah and Its Symbolism* (New York: Schocken, 1965), pp. 5–31. See also "Kabbalah and Myth," ibid., pp. 87–117.

4. See Daniel Matt, "The Mystic and the *Mizvot*," in *Jewish Spirituality I*, pp. 367–404 and further bibliography there. The vast Kabbalistic literature on *ta'amey ha-mizvot* was barely touched upon in I. Heinemann's classic work *Ta'amey ha-Mizvot be Sifrut Yisra'el* (Jerusalem: World Zionist Organization, 1959).

5. The roots of this dialectic are discussed in David Biale, *Gershom Scholem: Kabbalah and Counter-History*, 2d ed. (Cambridge, Mass.: Harvard University Press, 1987), pp. 78–82. See also the important material related to this subject contributed by Paul Mendes-Flohr at the beginning of his essay "Law and Sacrament: Ritual Observance in Twentieth-Century Jewish Thought," in *Jewish Spirituality II* (New York: Crossroad, 1987), pp. 321–22.

6. The anti-Hasidic polemical literature has been edited by Mordecai Wilensky in *Hasidim u-Mitnaggedim*, 2 vols. (Jerusalem: Mossad Bialik, 1970).

7. An extensive secondary literature on Hasidism is available in English. Unfortunately, there is no full history of the movement available, and even the one history accessible in Hebrew, S. Dubnov's *Toledot ha-Hasidut* (Tel Aviv: Dvir, 1960), is badly out of date. Introductory essays on Hasidism

can be found in B. Weinryb's *The Jews of Poland* (Philadelphia: Jewish Publication Society, 1972) p. 262ff. and in Gershom Scholem's *Major Trends in Jewish Mysticism* (New York: Schocken Books, 1941), p. 325ff. The spirit of early Hasidic devotion, at least for this reader, is perhaps best captured in Martin Buber's essay "The Life of the Hasidim," included in his *Hasidism and Modern Man* (New York: Harper and Row, 1966). Though this treatment by the young Buber suffers from excessive romanticism and the usual Buberian abstraction of Hasidic spirituality from its traditional moorings, it has a vitality lacking in most other Western presentations of the material. Two important collections of scholarly essays on Hasidism are Joseph Weiss, *Studies in Eastern European Jewish Mysticism* (Oxford: Oxford University Press, 1985) and Abraham J. Heschel, *The Circle of the Baal Shem Tov* (Chicago: University of Chicago Press, 1985). The present writer's contributions to this field include an exposition of how to study the Hasidic sources, "Teachings of the Hasidic Masters," in Barry W. Holtz, *Back to the Sources* (New York: Schocken Books, 1984); comments on theological innovation within Hasidism: "Hasidism: Discovery and Retreat" in Peter Berger, ed. *The Other Side of God* (Garden City, N.Y.: Anchor Press, 1981), and "Typologies of Leadership in Early Hasidism" in *Jewish Spirituality II* (New York: Crossroad, 1987).

8. See Raphael Mahler, *Hasidism and Haskalah* (Philadelphia: Jewish Publication Society, 1985).

9. The two major genres of Hasidic literature, homilies and tales, were both originally transmitted orally. Homilies were the first to be published, beginning in 1780 with the *Toledot Ya'aqov Yosef.* Much Hasidic theology was developed through these homilies, which were translated (often by memory some time after their delivery) by the author or a disciple from Yiddish into Hebrew. Tales were printed only much later, publication reaching its height in the late nineteenth and early twentieth century. They were often published in Yiddish and intended for a popular audience. I have discussed this in detail in "Teachings of the Hasidic Masters," in Holtz, ed., *Back to the Sources*, pp. 363–67.

10. The writings of Dov Baer include three major texts. *Maggid Devarav le-Ya'aqov*, first published in Korzec, 1781, is available in a critical edition by R. Schatz-Uffenheimer (Jerusalem: Magnes Press, 1976). Two other collections, available in traditional editions, are *Or Torah*, Korzec, 1804 and *Or ha-Emet*, Husiatyn, 1899. Teachings of Dov Baer are also reflected in such anonymous or otherwise attributed collections as *Liqqutim Yeqarim*, Lvov, 1792; *Kitvey Qodesh*, Lvov, 1862; *Keter Shem Tov*, Zolkiew, 1794/1795; and *Zava'at RYVaSH*, Zolkiew, n.d. Many works by the disciples of the Maggid are widely published and include most of the classics of Hasidic literature. Perhaps best known among these are the works of Levi Yizhak of Berdichev, Elimelech of Lezajsk, and Menahem Nahum of Chernobyl.

Shne'ur Zalman of Liadi, also a disciple of Dov Baer, developed his thought into the unique ḤaBaD system, which will be discussed below in section VII. The school of the Maggid has been treated in the important monograph *Ha-Hasidut Ke-Mystiqah* by R. Schatz-Uffenheimer (Jerusalem: Magnes Press, 1968), to which the present writer is much indebted.·

11. See discussion by Louis Jacobs in *Seeker of Unity* (New York: Basic Books, 1966), pp. 49–63. My own prior treatment of this theme in early Hasidic theology is found in Berger, ed., *The Other Side of God*, as cited in n. 7.

12. The question of mystical acosmicism versus mystical pantheism or immanentism was raised by Scholem in his critique of Martin Buber. See his "Martin Buber's Interpretation of Hasidism" in *The Messianic Idea in Judaism and Other Essays* (New York: Schocken Books, 1971), pp. 228–50; and Buber's reply, *Commentary* (September, 1963): 218–25. There is no question that Buber, especially in his early works, somewhat exaggerated the "world-embracing" quality of Hasidism, but evidence to support his reading is to be found both in such early works as *Me'or 'Eynayim* (see my translation in Menahem Nahum of Chernobyl, *Upright Practices and The Light of the Eyes* [New York: Paulist Press, 1982]), and in the writings of Polish Hasidic authors of the later period.

13. See J. G. Weiss, *"Talmud Torah le-Shiṭṭat Rabbi Israel BeSHT,"* in *Israel Brodie Festschrift*, Hebrew section (London: Jews' College, 1966).

14. These included especially, if quotation in the Hasidic sources is to be a guide, the *Zohar, Reshit Hokhmah* by Elijah De Vidas, *Shney Luḥot haBerit* by Isaiah Horowitz, and such secondary guides to the Lurianic system as Meir Poppers' *Peri 'Ez Ḥayyim* and Immanuel Hai Ricci's *Mishnat Hasidim*. These works and others like them were printed by the small-town Ukrainian Hebrew printing houses that catered primarily to a Hasidic clientele. This is another way of determining what works were popular among Hasidic audiences. The work by Horowitz was printed, for example, seven times in Russia/Poland between 1800 and 1860. The publications of these printers have been the subject of extensive bibliographical research in the writings of Chaim Lieberman, collected as *Ohel Rachel*, 3 vols., New York, 1980–1984.

15. Nahman of Bratslav, *Liqquṭey MoHaRaN* 20:2.

16. Cf. the materials on Ze'ev Wolf of Zhitomir, author of *Or ha-Me'ir*, discussed in J. G. Weiss, *Studies in Eastern European Jewish Mysticism* (Oxford: Oxford University Press, 1985), pp. 78–79.

17. This interpretation is widespread in early Hasidic sources. Cf. for example *Keter Shem Ṭov* (Brooklyn: Kehot, 1972), 26b, #204; *Liqqutim Yeqarim* (Jerusalem, 1974), 14b, #76, and the sources quoted in n. 54 ad loc. It is already found in the Kabbalistic writings of the late sixteenth-century *Yeqarim* (Jerusalem, 1974) 14b, #76, and the sources quoted in n. 54 ad loc.

(cf. Hayyim Vital's *Sha'ar ha-Mizvot*, Jerusalem, 1905, 33b) and possibly earlier. For a somewhat different reading of *li-shemah*, see also the article cited in n. 13 above, p. 154ff.

18. See Schatz-Uffenheimer, *Ha-Hasidut Ke-Mystiqah*, pp. 157–67.

19. The phrase is found in the opening paragraph of *Zava'at RYVaSH*, an anonymous collection of early Hasidic teachings that purports to be the testament of the Ba'al Shem Tov, first published Zolkiew, n.d. [179-?]. The same idea is found in widespread interpretations of Prov. 3:6, "Know Him in all your ways," scattered through early Hasidic literature. Cf. *Toledot Ya'aqov Yosef* (Korzec, 1780) 23b-c; *Maggid Devarav le-Ya'aqov* (ed. R. Schatz-Uffenheimer, 1976), pp. 95, 197.

20. Berger, ed., *The Other Side of God*, p. 125.

21. Yoma 28b.

22. See *Guide to the Perplexed*, ed. Pines, introduction, p. 9f; *Guide* 3:43 (p. 573); Mishnah Commentary 1:20–21.

23. An interesting and extreme example of this tendency is to be seen in the tales told by Rabbah bar bar Hanna (and others) as recorded in the Talmud, Baba Batra 73a-74b. These stories, mostly of sea monsters he had encountered on his travels, were taken to be of esoteric value if not of literal truth, and engendered a minor literature of commentary.

24. *Qedushat Levi ha-Shalem* (Jerusalem, 1958) 335b.

25. Makkot 23b is the talmudic *locus classicus* for the 613 commandments, including references to the limbs and the days of the solar year. See the various commentaries ad loc. (especially MaHaRSHA) for later explanations of these numbers. Louis Finkelstein (note to his edition of Sifre Devarim 76) suggests that the fixing of this number is Amoraic, the situation in Tannaitic times having been considerably more fluid. This view is supported by E. Urbach, *The Sages* (Jerusalem: Magnes Press, 1975), p. 343. Nahmanides is very aware of this in the opening remarks of his *hassagot* to Maimonides' *Sefer ha-Mizvot*, where he notes that strict adherence to the number 613 is an innovation of the Ge'onim. The number of 248 limbs in the body (without association to the commandments) is specified in Mishnah Ohalot 1:8. This number has been discussed by J. Preuss in his *Biblisch-Talmudische Medizin* (Berlin, 1923), p. 66ff. His claim that the number 248 is associated with the days of the lunar calendar seems to be without textual basis. See also the interesting if rather speculative suggestions by M. Bloch in *Revue des Etudes Juives* 1 (1880): 209f. E. Urbach dismisses Bloch's theory in *The Sages*, p. 837, n. 5. The correspondence R. Simlai suggests between the number of negative commandments and the days of the solar year should be seen in light of the strong inclination toward astrology among Babylonian Jews. (Simlai was a Babylonian who migrated to *Erez Yisrael*.) Cf. also the discussion of the numbers of the commandments by my colleague N. Danzig in *Sinai* 83 (1978): 153–58.

26. The number of 365 sinews in the body is already found in Targum J. to Gen. 1:27. Though we have no early source that connects this belief with the days of the solar year, the identity of these two numbers can hardly be coincidental. The parallel structures of cosmos, time, and individual soul, mentioned briefly in *Sefer Yezirah* and developed in *Sefer ha-Bahir* and elsewhere, may be reflected here. It was the medieval Kabbalists who first claimed that the negative as well as the positive commandments have their parallel within the human form. Cf. Zohar 1:170b and the other Zohar sources referred to by R. Margulies in *Sha'arey Zohar* (Jerusalem: Mossad Harav Kook, 1956) to Makkot 23b. This change is not yet found in the writings of Nahmanides and seems to originate in the late thirteenth century.

27. Another problem we moderns would have with such a teaching, that of the correspondence between universal human nature and the very specifically Jewish teachings of Torah, poses no difficulty for the Hasidic preacher. To him Jews and Judaism are the ultimate fulfillment of the human; how non-Jews answer the call of the inner limbs simply does not concern him.

28. See my article "On Translating Hasidic Homilies," *Prooftexts* 3:1 (1983): 63–72.

29. *Ma'or va-Shemesh* (Breslau, 1842), 256a.

30. The relationship between the inner limbs and sinews and the 613 commandments, to which we have already referred, is a commonplace of Hasidic homilies. Cf. *No'am Elimelech*, ed. Nigal, 61c, 80c; index s.v. *evarim*. The notion that each *mizvah* is "a limb of the *shekhinah*" is found in the *Maggid Devarav le-Ya'aqov* of Dov Baer of Miedzyrzec (ed. Schatz-Uffenheimer, 1976), section 32, p. 50. This idea goes back to those older Kabbalistic sources discussed by Scholem in *On the Kabbalah and Its Symbolism*, p. 44ff. Discussion of the *mizvot* in Hasidic sources begins with the *Toledot Ya'aqov Yosef* of Jacob Joseph of Polonnoye (Korzec, 1780), the first printed work of Hasidic teaching. In almost every weekly Torah portion Jacob Joseph digresses to discourse on a single commandment and its meaning in terms of Hasidic spirituality. Hasidic literature contains two well-known compendia of the commandments, in which the authors review each commandment and discuss its meaning. *Derekh Pequdekha* of Zvi Elimelech of Dinov (Lvov, 1851), divides each commandment into its ramifications in the realms of deed, speech, and thought, chiefly moralizing in the "thought" sections of most commandments. *Derekh Mizvotekha* of Menahem Mendel Schneersohn will be discussed below. Perhaps only in this latter work does a Hasidic author come close to showing the fascination with spiritually "locating" each aspect of the commandments that is so readily seen throughout the extensive Lurianic writings on this subject. In most of Hasidic literature, treatment of *ta'amey ha-mizvot* is sporadic and occurs

incidentally in homilies on the Torah portions in which the *mizvah* occurs or for a holiday on which a *mizvah* is observed.

31. See the statement by Meir ben Solomon ibn Sahula in the introduction to his commentary on *Sefer Yezirah*: . . . the path taken by those who, in our generation and in the preceding generations, for two hundred years, are called Kabbalists, *mequbbalim*, and they call the science of the ten *sefirot* and some of the reasons for the [biblical] commandments by the name of Kabbalah." This passage is quoted by Scholem in *Origins of the Kabbalah* (Philadelphia: Jewish Publication Society, 1987), p. 38.

32. Early Kabbalistic writings are replete with references to the *mizvot* and their meaning. The most important works of classical Kabbalah dealing specifically with the *mizvot* are *Sefer ha-Rimon* by Moses de Leon, ed. Elliot R. Wolfson (Decatur, Ga.: Scholars' Press, 1987), the *Ta'amey ha-Mizvot* of Joseph of Hamadam (part one edited in Brandeis University Ph.D. diss., 1974, of Menachem Meier; part two, on the negative commandments, remains in manuscript), the anonymous *Ra'aya Mehemna*, published as part of the printed Zohar editions, and the *Ta'amey ha-Mizvot* of Menahem of Recanati (Constantinople, 1544). Cf. the discussion by Daniel Matt in *Jewish Spirituality I*, p. 381, to which I have referred in n. 4 above.

33. See Lawrence Fine, "The Contemplative Practice of *Yihudim* in Lurianic Kabbalah" in *Jewish Spirituality II*, pp. 64–98, and Louis Jacobs, "The Uplifting of Sparks in Later Jewish Mysticism," ibid., pp. 99–126.

34. I do not mean to oversimplify. The multiplication of *sefirot* had begun before Luria. 10 x 4 for 4 worlds is widespread outside Lurianic Kabbalah. On the origin of the "four worlds" image in fourteenth-century Kabbalah, see Scholem in *Tarbiz* 2 (1931): 415ff. and 3 (1932): 33ff. The idea that each of the *sefirot* also includes all the others is found in Cordoveran as well as Lurianic texts, and its source is earlier, in the immediate post-Zohar literature. See Scholem's discussion in *Kiryat Sefer* 1 (1924): 48, and cf. the discussion by Y. Ben-Shelomo in *Torat ha-Elohut shel Rabbi Moshe Cordovero* (Jerusalem: Mossad Bialik, 1965), p. 248 and n. 232. The reconfiguration of the ten *sefirot* into five *parzufim* first takes place in the latter sections of the Zohar called *idrot*. See the introductory discussion by Scholem in *Major Trends in Jewish Mysticism*, pp. 269–73.

35. Among those who accused philosophers of being lax in observance were Jonah Gerondi, Jacob ben Sheshet, Shalom Ashkenazi, and Moses de Leon. See Matt in *Jewish Spirituality I*, pp. 374–75; Yitzhak Baer, *A History of the Jews in Christian Spain*, vol. 1 (Philadelphia: Jewish Publication Society, 1978), pp. 240, 250, and Bernard Septimus, *Hispano-Jewish Culture in Transition* (Cambridge: Harvard University Press, 1982), pp. 93–95.

36. *No'am Elimelech* 43a-b, 88a.

37. Shabbat 31a.

38. While the Tannaim were able to find reasons and principles behind

many commandments, there were some, such as the red heifer and the levirate marriage, that they were at a loss to explain. These so-called *ḥuqqim* (statutes) were nevertheless considered beneficial because their observance was said to refine human character and bring opportunities for reward. In the Middle Ages, this discussion is continued by Saadya Gaon, who divides the laws into two categories—those of reason (*sikhliyot*) and those of revelation (*shim'iyot*). Our author refers to these two kinds of laws as *mizvot* and *ḥuqqim*. See Urbach, *The Sages*, pp. 365–80; and Saadya Gaon: *Book of Doctrines and Beliefs*, in *Three Jewish Philosophers*, ed. Alexander Altmann (New York: Atheneum, 1969), pp. 94–102.

39. Tanḥuma Ḥuqqat 8.

40. Niddah 61b. Also see discussion by W. D. Davies, *Torah in the Messianic Age and/or the Age to Come* (Philadelphia: Society of Biblical Literature, 1952), pp. 65, 80, 82.

41. *Peri ha-Arez*: 6a-b (*Toledot*).

42. The original Hasidic source is *Maggid Devarav le-Ya'aqov* (ed. Schatz-Uffenheimer, p. 132f.): "The *zaddiq*, through his good deeds, makes an impression above and causes joy for the upper worlds. For example, the patriarchs did with the wells and the staffs the same acts [*pe'ulot*] as are done through *tefillin*. When the patriarchs performed those acts they were attached chiefly to [*'iqqar hilqasherulam hayah be-*] the contemplative universe. When he saw a well, for example, he became attached to the source of living waters, to the river that flows forth from Eden. Contemplation is a high mountain; objects [*'uvedot*; "events" or "things"] are pointers to it." The point is that for the patriarchs all that they encountered served as a symbolic reminder of the sefirotic world. Such a view stands at the very basis of Kabbalistic symbolism and its reintroduction of natural symbols into Judaism. It is adumbrated frequently in prescriptive fashion in the early sources of Hasidism: "Whatever a person sees should remind him of divinity" (*Zava'at RYVaSH* [Cracow, 1896], 3b). In this sense the patriarchs seem to be different only in that they do not yet have the *specific* pointers to divinity that are the *mizvot*. The idea that spiritual intensity needs some expression in the realm of deed is also well-documented in Hasidic sources. See the passages quoted by R. Schatz-Uffenheimer in *Ha-Hasidut ke-Mystiqah*, p. 75ff.

43. While the theurgic *kavvanot* of prayer are largely abandoned in Hasidism (cf. the treatment in Weiss, *Studies in Eastern European Jewish Mysticism*, p. 98ff.), *kavvanot* directly related to performance of the *mizvot* were retained at least in circles close to the *zaddiqim* themselves. This distinction between *kavvanot ha-tefillah* and *kavvanot ha-mizvot* is made explicitly in the passage by Meshullam Feibush Heller of Zbarash translated by Weiss, p. 113. A *kavvanah* for ablutions in the *miqveh* on Sabbath eve, attributed to the Ba'al Shem Tov himself, has been published frequently

(cf. *Kedushat Levi ha-Shalem*, p. 329). The language of this brief text is simple and direct, in contrast to most pre-Hasidic *kavvanot*. This is less true of the *kavvanot* for *teqi'at shofar* attributed to the BeSHT in *Shemu'ah Tovah* (Warsaw, 1938), 76ff. and reprinted in *Keter Shem Tov* (Brooklyn: Kehot, 1972), addenda, pp. 5–7. These seem to belong quite fully to the Lurianic tradition and may not be original to the Ba'al Shem Tov at all. Hasidic tales abound in testimony to the continued use of some sort of *kavvanot* for such ritual acts as blowing the shofar, waving the lulav, and eating of matzah at the seder meal. *Shivḥey ha-BeSHT*, ed. Horodezky (Berlin: Ajanoth, 1922), p. 101 mentions a *"kavvanah* for eating" practiced by the BeSHT at a festive meal.

44. *Degel Maḥaneh Ephraim* 86d-87a (*Va-era*).

45. The term literally means "the handing over of the soul" and refers specifically to devotion unto death. This term and concept have played a major role in Jewish religious thought throughout a history in which martyrdom was all too often a reality Jews had to face. Its origins are in the Maccabean period, as attested by the Books of Daniel, Judith, and the Maccabees, but it was called forth again during the Hadrianic persecutions, the crusades, the inquisition, the Chmielnicki massacres, and at many less-known junctures in Jewish history. *Mesirut nefesh* has been studied by a great many Jewish historians, including Yizhak Baer, Jacob Katz, and Azriel Shochat. The place of *mesirut nefesh* in the thought of Rabbi Nahman of Bratslav has been treated by J. G. Weiss in his *Meḥqarim be-Ḥasidut Braslav* (Jerusalem: Mossad Bialik, 1974) p. 172ff. The distinctive interpretation of this concept in ḤaBaD thought has been the subject of a most important doctoral dissertation by H. J .T. C. Loewenthal, "The Concept of Mesirat Nefesh ('Self Sacrifice') in the Teachings of R. Dov Baer of Lubavitch," University of London, 1981. The introduction to that dissertation contains a brief history of the concept and (p. 15, n. 26) a full bibliography of the scholarly treatments.

46. *Ba-'ayin mamash*. The capitalization of "Nought" indicates that *ayin* for the Hasidic author refers to the highest realm within divinity.

47. The image of being "lacking a limb" to describe one whose devotional life is unwhole is found elsewhere in early Hasidism, and is attributed to the Ba'al Shem Tov. See *Ẕava'at RYVaSH* (Cracow, 1896), 4b; *Liqquṭim Yeqarim* (Jerusalem, 1974), 2. It is precisely the sort of earthy metaphor that might well have been used by the BeSHT. For the roots of this notion in earlier Jewish mysticism, see Scholem's "The Meaning of Torah in Jewish Mysticism" in *On the Kabbalah and Its Symbolism* (New York: Schocken, 1969) p. 50ff. Cf. also in n. 83 below.

48. Underlying this statement is the rabbinic tradition that distinguishes Moses' prophecy from that of all others by claiming that "All other prophets saw through a glass darkly, but Moses saw [or 'prophesied'] through a glass brightly," Yebamot 49b. Both philosophers and Kabbalists made extensive

use of this rubric throughout the Middle Ages. Levi Yizhak's claim that the one who serves through *mesirut nefesh* sees God without any glass at all (Is there a play on words here between *ba-'ayin mamash*—"indeed in the *Nought*"—*and ba-'ayin mamash*—"with his very eye"?) is indeed extreme. Such bold usages, contrasting sharply with the conservative language of most earlier Kabbalists, are not unusual in the Hasidic sources.

49. *Kedushat Levi Ha-Shalem*, 15ff.

50. Bereshit Rabbah 43:6. Typically, the word *sod* ('secret') is not found in the Midrash, but is added in the Hasidic quotation.

51. This understanding of Hasidism as a social phenomenon, generally attributed to the discussion by Jacob Katz in *Tradition and Crisis* (New York: Schocken Books, 1971), p. 231ff., is widely accepted among students of the movement.

52. Biblical commentators have suggested that this verse is post-Deuteronomic, to be dated much later than those verses around it. See Gerhard von Rad, *Genesis: A Commentary* (Philadelphia: Westminster Press, 1972), pp. 270–71, and Claus Westermann, *Genesis 12–36: A Commentary* (Minneapolis: Augsburg Publishing House, 1985), pp. 424–25. John Von Seters' *Abraham in History and Tradition* (New Haven: Yale University Press, 1975), p. 273 suggests that this verse, along with other portions of the Abrahamic narratives, reflects Deuteronomic influence.

53. See 2 Baruch 57 and further citations by S. Sandmel, "Philo's Place in Judaism," part II, *HUCA* 26 (1955): 156f.

54. *De Abrahamo*, a part of Philo's Exposition, deals chiefly with the literal Abraham; the allegorical Abraham is the chief subject of *De Migratione*. The two, however, are not clearly distinguishable. See Sandmel, as quoted in the succeeding note, pp. 217f. and 225.

55. "Philo's Place in Judaism," Part I, *HUCA* 25 (1954): 209–37; Part 2, *HUCA* 26 (1955: 151–332. References below are all to part 2.

56. *De Abr.* 167–207; Sandmel, p. 245ff.

57. Sandmel, p. 259ff.

58. Op. cit., p. 228.

59. *De Abr.* 5.

60. Ibid., p. 231. Cf. also p. 312.

61. Sandmel, p. 287 and n. 299.

62 . *De Migratione Abrahami* 92–93.

63. See E. P. Sanders, *Paul and Palestinian Judaism* (Philadelphia: Fortress Press, 1977), pp. 552–56; Erwin R. Goodenough, *By Light, Light* (New Haven: Yale University Press, 1935), pp. 398, 900ff; id., "Paul and the Hellenization of Christianity," in *Religions in Antiquity*, ed. Jacob Neusner (Leiden: E. J. Brill, 1968); Samuel Sandmel, *The Genius of Paul* (Philadelphia: Fortress Press, 1979), pp. 8–15, 53–55; *Paul and Rabbinic Judaism* (Philadelphia: Fortress Press, 1980), pp. 28, 93–98, 151. These views do not deal

specifically with Paul's views on Abraham.

64. Of course there exists a vast literature on Paul and the Law, including scientific studies by such luminaries as Albert Schweitzer, Rudolf Bultmann, W. D. Davies, and Sandmel. A full bibliography may be found in E. P. Sanders, *Paul and Palestinian Judaism* (Philadelphia: Fortress Press, 1977), p. 557ff., whose views I have found most illuminating and have generally followed in this brief treatment.

65. *Contra Trypho* 46:3–4, 67:7–8, *et passim*.

66. This connection was first made by M. Joel, *Blicke in die Religionsgeschichte* 11, p. 174, as noted by Bernard Bamberger in "Revelation of Torah After Sinai," *HUCA* 16 (1941): 97ff.

67. See S. Lieberman, ad loc.; *Tosefta ki-Feshuṭah*, vol. 8, p. 986f.

68. Urbach, *The Sages*, p. 318 (see n. 25).

69. Bereshit Rabbah 49:2; 64:4. Some other rabbinic sources for Abraham's observance of the commandments are Nedarim 32a, Yerushalmi Qiddushin 4:12, Va-yiqra Rabbah 2:10, Tanḥuma Lekh Lekha 1, ibid., 10, Tanḥuma Buber Va-yiggash 12, Avot de-Rabbi Nathan I, ed. Schechter, p. 94, Yalqut Jeremiah 321, Yalqut Tehillim 871.

70. Baba Meẓia 87a; Bereshit Rabbah 79:7. Other examples of patriarchal observance of the Law are listed in Sandmel, op. cit., p. 207f.

71. Cf. Ginzberg, *Legends of the Jews*, vol. 5, p. 295, n. 167.

72. Bereshit Rabbah 95:3.

73. See the sources collected in these categories in Strack-Billerbeck, *Kommentar zum neuen Testament aus Talmud und Midrasch*, p. 205f. Of course the lines between them are not to be drawn too rigidly. If God called upon Abraham's innards to reveal Torah to him, the revelation may be said to come from God as well as from within himself.

74. *Pesikta de-Rab Kahana, ba-Ḥodesh*, ed. Mandelbaum (New York: Jewish Theological Seminary, 1962), vol. 1, pp. 202–4.

75. No treatment of Abraham as portrayed in medieval Jewish literature yet exists. Such an essay, parallel to Sandmel's treatment of Abraham in the Philonic corpus, would be a most interesting contribution to Jewish scholarship. On Abraham who "discovered the true faith by meditating on nature," etc., see the Hellenistic and rabbinic sources quoted in Ginzberg, *Legends of the Jews*, vol. 5, p. 210, n. 16.

76. *Guide for the Perplexed* 3:51, trans. Shlomo Pines (Chicago: University of Chicago Press, 1969), pp. 623–24.

77. *Mishneh Kesef*, Pressburg, 1905, p. 71ff. Quoted passage is on p. 72.

78. *Targum RaSaG la-Torah*, ed. Zucker (New York: Jewish Theological Seminary, 1984), p. 427.

79. Judah ben Barzilai of Barcelona, *Perush Sifer Yezirah* (Berlin: Meqiẓey Nirdamim, 1885), p. 59.

80. Ibn Ezra on Gen. 26:5, Lev. 19:19, *Yesod Mora'* chap. 5 (Frankfurt,

1840), p. 22f. See also Ibn Ezra's comments on the patriarchs and their relationship to the commandments there in *Yesod Mora.'*

81. See RaMBaN on Gen. 15:2, 15:17, 17:1, etc. See also F. Talmage, "Apples of Gold," in *Jewish Spirituality I*, p. 337ff.

82. RaMBaN's commentary on the Torah, ed. Chavel (Jerusalem: Mossad Harav Kook, 1959), p. 6. See also Scholem's discussion in "The Meaning of Torah in Jewish Mysticism" in *On the Kabbalah and Its Symbolism*, p. 38ff. On the Primordial Torah, see the extensive discussion and sources quoted in Heschel, *Torah Min ha-Shamayim*, vol. 2 (London: Soncino Press, 1975), pp. 8–12.

83. Nahmanides' well-known views on this subject were probably influenced by Judah Ha-Levi, who claimed that the Torah was best and most appropriately observed in the Land of Israel (*Kuzari*, 5:23). On Nahmanides, cf. C. R. Chavel, *Rabbi Moshe ben Nahman* (Jerusalem: Mossad Harav Kook, 1973), pp. 198–200.

84. See Bahya's *Commentary.* ed. Chavel (Jerusalem: Mossad Harav Kook, 1982) vol. I, p. 228. Bahya's use of this term follows that by the author of *Sod 'Ez ha-Da'at* (probably Ezra ben Solomon of Gerona): "Therefore our sages of blessed memory said that the patriarchs fulfilled the Torah contemplatively (*be-sikhlam*)." This text is printed in Gershom Scholem's *Pirqey Yesod* (Jerusalem: Mossad Bialik, 1976), p.195. On the multi-leveled relationship to truth, cf. the discussion in Talmage, p. 315ff. The question of patriarchal observance of the commandments is also discussed by Rabbi Solomon ben Abraham Adret (c. 1235–c. 1310), whose halakhic and theological opinions were much influenced by Nahmanides. In his *Responsa* (#94), Adret raises the question of Jacob's seeming violation of the Law by marrying two sisters. He goes on to discuss the *aggadah* that Abraham fulfilled the entire Torah, admonishing the questioner "not to be surprised, since you have already come to know that there is not a single specific in the *mizvot* which does not point to some wise matter. Wisdom itself then obligates the lower creatures to be commanded concerning both actions to be done and those to be avoided. These deeds and avoidances themselves proclaim the wisdom hidden within them. It was by their great wisdom that the patriarchs attained to these principles." Here the word *hokhmah* is still used in its pre-Kabbalistic sense of "wisdom" or "intellect," but the transition to *hokhmah* as the divine "realm" that is the source of Torah and commandments is not far off.

85. *Me'irat 'Eynayim* 42:9ff.

86. It seems that Bahya is here referring to the passage quoted above from *Guide* 3:51. The wording of his interpretation leaves some room for ambiguity; the use of '*im* ('with') probably means that God can be served while one is also tending the flocks or working at other matters, as Maimonides says in the aforementioned passage. In that case Bahya is reading

Exodus 20:9 (*sheshet yamim ta'avod ve-'asita kol melakhtekha*) to mean: "On the six days you may serve [God] along with doing all your labor." It is not implausible, but somewhat less likely, that *'im* in this passage should be translated "through" or "by means of" rather than "along with."

87. Bahir, ed. Scholem #132. See Scholem's brief discussion of this passage in *Origins of the Kabbalah* (Philadelphia: Jewish Publication Society, 1987) p. 146.

88. *Sha'arey Orah*, ed. Ben Shelomo (Jerusalem: Mossad Bialik, 1970) vol. 2, p. 37f. The idea of Creation through *ḥesed* is based on an *aggadah* found in Bereshit Rabbah 12:15 and quoted by RaSHI to Gen. 1:1. The reference there is to *middat ha-raḥamim*, which is not distinguished from *middat ha-ḥesed* in the rabbinic sources. The reference to the fiery furnace is to the aggadic account of Nimrod's punishment of the young Abraham. See the sources referred to in Ginzberg, *Legends of the Jews*, vol. 5, p. 212ff. Gikatilla's opening phrase in referring to Abraham is based on *Sefer Yezirah*, 6:7.

89. Zohar I:99b *et seq.*

90. Zohar 3:13b. Note the precise converse to the Pauline Abraham in this reading! Paul's Abraham is praiseworthy because he has *faith before* circumcision; the rabbinic Abraham is worthy because he has *Torah after* circumcision.

91. As quoted in Abraham Azulai's *Or ha-Ḥamah* ad loc.; ed. Prszemysl f. II b. The word *'orlah* ("foreskin") is widely used by way of analogy to refer to various aspects of the forbidden or the defiled. This extended usage may be seen as early as Lev. 19:23, creating the widespread rabbinic usage of *'orlah* to refer to fruits of trees in their first three years, and in several biblical passages referring metaphorically to the *'orlah* of the heart (Lev. 26:41, Deut. 10:16, Jer. 9:25, etc.). In Kabbalah, *'orlah* becomes a synonym for the force of evil, that which seeks to hide the "fruit" or the organ of generation which will bear fruit in its union with the *shekhinah*.

92. Cf. Nedarim 32a; Yalqut Jeremiah 321.

93. Cf. *Sha'arey Orah*, vol. I, pp. 58, 63, 78, interpreting Gen. 12:2.

94. Zohar 3:276b, Ra'aya Mehemna. I am emending the opening line to read *le-gabbey* rather than the printed versions' *le-gabbakh*. The relationships here are not quite clearly stated. It seems best to say that the earthly Abraham was a foster father [*oman*] to the *shekhinah* because his correspondent above, Abraham as *ḥesed* in the sefirotic world, is her "actual" father.

95. For the many Zohar references to this theme see the sources quoted in R. Margulies, *Sha'arey Zohar* (Jerusalem: Mossad Harav Kook, 1978) s. v. Makkot 23b.

96. See Hasdai Crescas, *Biṭṭul 'Iqqarey ha-Noẓrim* 6:2, as quoted by I. Heinemann, *Ta'amey ha-Mizvot be-Sifrut Yisra'el*, p. 102.

97. *Sefer Yuḥasin*, quoted by MaHaRSHA to Yoma 28a.

98. Ed. Venice, 1583, f. 84.

99. See Eugene Newman, *Life and Teachings of Isaiah Horowitz* (London, 1972) and the treatment by S. A. Horodezky in *Ha-Mistorin be-Yisra'el* (Tel Aviv: Aggudat ha-Sofrim, 1961), pp. 54–113.

100. *Shney Luḥot ha-Berit*, part two, introduction to Torah commentary (Jerusalem, 1959, v. 2, p. 52). See also the sermonic work *'Arvey Naḥal* by the Hasidic preacher David Solomon Eibenschuetz of Soroki (Sudilkow, 1835), *Toledot*, which directly quotes this passage, showing clearly (though such evidence is hardly needed) that the passage was read in Hasidic circles.

101. Scholem, *Major Trends in Jewish Mysticism*, p. 338.

102. See Scholem's discussion of these ideas in "The Meaning of the Torah in Jewish Mysticism," in *On the Kabbalah and Its Symbolism*, pp. 66ff, 78 and with regard to their specific use in Sabbatian theology in "Redemption Through Sin" in *The Messianic Idea in Judaism*, p. 111ff.

103. A particularly powerful example of such thinking is found in *Sidduro shel Shabbat* by Hayyim of Chernovtsy, a well-known rabbi and author who was influenced by Dov Baer of Miedzyrzec and his school:

> At a time of true love, desire, and attachment to the blessed Creator, one becomes completely detached from human reality. . . . Then even fulfillment of the Torah is irrelevant [*lo shayyakh*], because the passion of attachment is so great. This is like the case of a father and his much-loved only son who have not seen one another for many years. When they see one another face to face they embrace and kiss with a love that is as strong as death, their souls going out to one another. All their other senses cease to exist, just like in the moment of death. This is the love that Israel should have for their Creator, blessed be He and His name, a love of such great passion and desire, since they are a part of Him. But if they were constantly in this state there would be no Torah. One who has left the bounds of humanity can fulfill no *mizvah* and can study no Torah. That is why God put it into our nature that we be cut off and fall back from too much love. Then Torah can be fulfilled. (chap. 7, section 1:16; ed. Jerusalem, 1960, f. 81a).

Compare this to the passages quoted by Schatz-Uffenheimer in *ḤaḤasidut ke-Mystiqah*, pp. 71, 76.

104. For a systematic approach to major themes in Bratslav thought, see Appendix 1, "Faith, Doubt, and Reason" in my *Tormented Master, A Life of Rabbi Nahman of Bratslav* (Tuscaloosa: University of Alabama Press, 1979). See also the major study by Joseph Weiss, "Ha-Qushiya be-Torat Rabbi Nahman mi-Bratslav" in his *Meḥqarim be-Ḥasidut Braslav* (Jerusalem: Bialik Institute, 1974), p. 109ff. The best systematic treatment of ḤaBaD thought is that by Rachel Elior, *The Theory of Divinity of Ḥasidut ḤaBaD* (Jerusalem: Magnes Press, 1982) in Hebrew. Also see her *The Paradoxical Ascent to God: The Kabbalistic Theosophy of Habad Hasidism* (New York: SUNY Press, 1993). An English summary of her work is "ḤaBaD, the Contemplative Ascent

to God," in *Jewish Spirituality II*, pp. 157–205. I am much indebted to Elior's work for my understanding of ḤaBaD. Also still useful on ḤaBaD thought is Jacobs, *Seeker of Unity*, mentioned above in n. 11.

105. That is the Hebrew title of his article which appeared in English as "Contemplative Mysticism and 'Faith' in Hasidic Piety," *Journal of Jewish Studies* 4 (1953):19–29, reprinted in his *Studies in Eastern European Jewish Mysticism*, pp. 43–55.

106. *Liqqutey Halakhot* was composed over a long period of time. Bratslav tradition claims that Nathan began the work while his master was still alive (i.e., before 1810), though the sources do not unequivocally support this view. Descriptions of Nathan's last days in 1845 do indicate that he continued to work on the *Halakhot* until the end of his life. See the materials collected in N. Z. Koenig's *Neveh Ẓaddiqim* (Beney Beraq, 1969), p. 87ff. The lengthy and often repetitious text gives indications that Nathan did not write it in consecutive order, but rather over the years went back to sections already completed and added to them freely. This tendency was encouraged by the fact that for a long portion of Nathan's career (from 1826), the governmental decree against the printing of Kabbalistic and Hasidic books in Russia prevented publication of Nathan's writings. Only the first section of *Liqqutey Halakhot* on *Oraḥ ḥayyim* was published during Nathan's lifetime, in Jassy, Wallachia (then a Turkish province), 1843. These volumes were smuggled across the border for distribution among the Bratslav *ḥasidim*, who lived almost entirely within the Russian border. The remaining portions of the work were published in Zolkiew and Lvov between 1847 and 1861.

Menahem Mendel Scheersohn was known primarily as a halakhic authority. His highly respected responsa were published in Vilna beginning in 1871 (*She'elot u-Teshuvot Ẓemaḥ Ẓedeq*). *Derekh Mizvotekha*, however, was printed only in the twentieth century (Poltava, 1911–12). A bibliography of Menahem Mendel's writings is published as a supplement to the new edition of his responsa, section *Oraḥ Hayyim*, Brooklyn, 1945.

107. Shne'ur Zalman attempts to show the student exactly where he stands in the process of development. There is a great emphasis, particularly in the popular *Tanya*, on detailed labelling and description of the various stages in the growth of religious consciousness. In this Shne'ur Zalman stands in the tradition of pre-Hasidic works of Kabbalistic ethics. This is psychologically very different than the "smash the lock" ethos that prevailed in some other early Hasidic circles. Systematic inculcation of religious ideas and devotional values went hand in hand in Lubavich with an attempt to control the wild enthusiasm of the early Hasidic milieu. See the discussion of the Hasidic outbursts of 1770 in the writings of Rabbi Joseph Isaac of Lubavich as well as the letter of Rabbi Yizhak Isaac Epstein of Homel, translated by Louis Jacobs in *Seeker of Unity*.

108. *'Iggerot ha-Qodesh*, appended to Kalisker's *Ḥesed le-Avraham*, #37.

109. *Liqqutey MoHaRaN 33:4*.

110. Ibid., 22:10.

111. On God's own observance of the commandments, cf. Soṭah 14a; Berakhot 6a, 7a; and Jer. Bikkurim 1:3 (65c). This motif has been discussed by Arthur Marmorstein in *The Doctrine of Merits in Old Rabbinic Literature*, vol. 2 (New York: Ktav, 1968), pp. 62–68.

112. *Liqqutey MoHaRaN* II:78.

113. I have discussed this teaching in *Tormented Master*, p. 263ff. For my understanding of this teaching and its importance, I remain thankful to Jeffrey Dekro.

114. *Derekh erez*, the student of Nahman will recall, also alludes to *derekh erez yisra'el*, the point at which he determined that he could still observe the commandments spiritually even if forced to violate them physically. See *Tormented Master*, pp. 77, 85, 263 and my article in Berger, *The Other Side of God*, p. 129.

115. Referring to the day when all the nations will abandon idolatry and call on the one God.

116. The associations here are based on those made by Nahman in *Liqqutey MoHaRaN* 65:3. The "one" of "Hear O Israel" is the ultimate oneness of all being, in which there is no distinction between the good and ill that seem to befall us in this world. Nahman refers to the rabbinic dictum (Pesaḥim 50a) that in the future we will thank God as "the one who is and does good" for all that happens to us.

117. Berakhot 15a.

118. Following a Lurianic view that *qelipot* hide but contain the good, without which they would not be sustained. The mystic's discovery of oneness destroys the *qelipah*, in this case the foreign language, that hides the kernel of light.

119. BT Sanhedrin 4b.

120. M. Berachot 1:1, 1:2. Discussion in BT 2b-4b.

121. *Liqqutey MoHaRaN 52*.

122. Typically for Bratslav thought, it is suffering that leads one to transcendence. Only by confronting the emotional conflicts with which every person is plagued can we come to the longing for God that will lead us to true transcendence. The chief example for this path in Bratslav is the life of the master himself. See *Tormented Master*, p. 15f and chapters 1, 3, and 4, *passim*. The contrast between Bratslav and ḤaBaD on this point is especially marked. See below.

123. The concluding section of *Adon 'Olam*, a hymn recited as part of the bedtime *shema'* liturgy.

124. *Liqqutey Halakhot, Oraḥ Ḥayyim, Hilkhot qeri'at shema'* 1; ed. Jerusalem, 1963, p. 210.

125. *Tormented Master*, p. 285ff.

126. Cf. the continuation of the passage just quoted from *Liqqutey Halakhot*: "The essence of perfection is in the return from [the state of] negation, contracting the light [so that it fit] into measures and vessels." Such admonitions are frequent in Nathan's work, which is wary of a flight into mystical fantasy that ignores or seeks to flee from the struggle for self-perfection, cast largely in moralistic terms.

127. Abraham Joshua Heschel, *The Circle of the Baal Shem Tov* (Chicago: University of Chicago Press, 1985), p. 21.

128. That seems to be the most appropriate term to characterize the homilies collected in such works as his *Torah Or* (Kapust, 1836), *Liqqutey Torah* (Zhitomir, 1848), *Ma'amarim TaQSaB* (Brooklyn, 1964), and elsewhere. While the homiletic form is maintained, it becomes largely incidental to the exposition of ideas and elaboration of Shne'ur Zalman's unique usage of Kabbalistic terminology.

129. The terms *sovev* and *memale'* (found in chapters 48 and 51 of the *Tanya* and widely in the later published homilies of Shne'ur Zalman) are adapted by Shne'ur Zalman from Lurianic sources. Cf. the note by Elior in *Theory of Divinity of Hasidut HaBaD*, p. 34, n. 44. His use of these terms, however, goes far beyond that intended in the Lurianic sources, and is partially influenced by Cordoveran thinking, as Elior shows.

130. See the fuller treatment of these two types of service in Elior, *Jewish Spirituality*, pp. 178–81.

131. Cf. the discussion of Schatz-Uffenheimer, *Ha-Hasidut Ke-Mystiqah*, pp. 14–18, 54–58, index s.v. *'Avodah bi-Gashmiyut*.

132. Cf. the treatment by Schatz-Uffenheimer, *"Anti-spiritualism be-Hasidut,"* in *Molad* 171 (1962): 513–28.

133. *Tanya*, chap. 12.

134. The inner relationship of thought, speech, and action is inherited by Hasidism from earlier works of Jewish theology. A contemporaneous non-HaBaD Hasidic treatment of the commandments, *Derekh Piqudekha* (Lvov, 1851) by Zvi Elimelech Shapira of Dynov in fact divides each commandment into these three sections, finding a contemplative, verbal, and concrete active aspect to each of the *mizvot*.

135. Ed. Poltava, 1911–12, f. 28a-29b. I have taken some minor liberties, including changes from third to second person, to render the text comprehensible to the English reader.

136. Shabbat 31a.

137. This was supposedly the personal custom of Rabbi Isaac Luria. See *Sefer ha-Kavvanot*, n.p., 1729[!], 2a and Jacob Zemah's *Nagid u-Mezavveh* (Jerusalem, 1965), p. 40. The passage there refers to "accepting upon oneself the positive commandment" of love of neighbor before praying. The conversion of this intent into an actual declaration preceding the

morning service is already found in the various eighteenth-century recensions of the Lurianic liturgy (R. Shabbatai of Raszkow, R. Asher Margulies, etc.). The commandment is taken by the above-quoted passages to refer both to the love of all Israel and to the specific love among the *ḥaverim*, companions in the study of Kabbalistic lore.

138. *Liqqutey Torah . . . Ta'amey ha-Miẓvot*, Vilna, 1880, 77a. Though attributed to Hayyim Vital, this book is actually a part of Meir Poppers' *Peri 'Eẓ Hayyim*.

139. See Scholem's discussion of this motif in *Sabbatai Sevi* (Princeton: Princeton University Press, 1973), pp. 49, 302–3.

140. Note how Menahem Mendel has made creative use of a concept with which we are already familiar: that of unwhole service producing a deformed result. See above, n. 47. Now the service of any Jew, no matter how impassioned, that does not contain within it the presence of all Israel is said to be "deformed."

141. Elior, "ḤaBaD: The Contemplative Ascent to God," in *Jewish Spirituality II*, pp. 160–73.

142. M. Avot 5:10.

143. From the daily liturgy, *Sim Shalom*.

144. Zohar 2:135a.

145. See Michael Stanislawski, *Tsar Nicolas I and the Jews* (Philadelphia: Jewish Publication Society, 1983), p. 150ff. From a Hasidic rather than a scholarly point of view, see Joseph Isaac Schneersohn, *The Tsemaḥ Tsedek and the Haskalah Movement* (Brooklyn, N.Y.: Kehot, 1946).

146. See Martin Buber's chapter, "Symbolic and Sacramental Existence" in *The Origin and Meaning of Hasidism* (New York: Horizon, 1960), pp. 152–81.

147. The accusation was made by Abraham Kalisker. See the *'Iggerot ha-Qodesh* appended to Kalisker's *Ḥesed le-Avraham*, 37. Cf. the discussion in my *Tormented Master*, p. 97f.; p. 124, n. 9.

Bibliography

I. *Traditional and Hasidic Authors**

Abraham of Kalisk. *Ḥesed le-Avraham*. Chernovtsy, 1851.

Azulai, Abraham. *Or ha-Ḥamah*. Przemysl, 1896–98.

De Leon, Moses. *Sefer ha-Rimon*. Edited by Elliot R. Wolfson. Decatur, Ga.: Scholars' Press, 1987.

De Vidas, Elijah. *Reshit Ḥokhmah*. Venice, 1579.

Dov Baer of Linitz. *Shivḥey ha-BeSHT*. Edited by Shmuel Abba Horodezky. Berlin: Ajanoth, 1922.

Dov Baer of Miedzyrzec. *Maggid Devarav le-Ya'aqov*. Korzec, 1781.

___. *Or ha-Emet*. Husiatyn, 1899.

___. *Or Torah*. Korzec, 1804.

Elimelech of Lezajsk. *No'am Elimelech*. Edited by Gedalyah Nigal. Jerusalem: Mossad Harav Kook, 1978.

Epstein, Kalonymos Kalman. *Ma'or va-Shemesh*. Breslau, 1842.

Gikatilla, Joseph. *Sha'arey Orah*. Edited by Yosef Ben Shelomo. Jerusalem: Mossad Bialik, 1970.

Ha-Levi, Judah. *Kuzari* (1506). Tel Aviv, 1948.

Hayyim of Chernovtsy. *Sidduro shel Shabbat*. Mohilev, 1813.

Horowitz, Isaiah. *Shney Luḥot ha-Berit*. Amsterdam, 1648–49.

Ibn Ezra, Abraham. *Yesod Mora'* (*1530*). Frankfurt, 1840.

Ibn Kaspi, Joseph. *Mishneh Kesef*. Pressburg, 1905.

Isaac of Acre. *Me'irat 'Eynayim*. Edited by Amos Goldreich. Jerusalem: Akademon, 1984.

Jacob Joseph of Polonnoye. *Toledot Ya'aqov Yosef*. Korzec, 1780.

*Classical rabbinic and anonymous medieval works are not listed.

Joseph of Hamadam. *Ta'amey ha-Mizvot*. Part one, edited by Menachem Meier. Ph.D. dissertation, Brandeis University, 1974. Part two, on the negative commandments, is currently being edited by Leora Sachs Shmuely in a dissertation at Bar Ilan University.

Judah ben Barzilai of Barcelona. *Perush Sefer Yezirah*. Berlin: Meqizey Nirdamim, 1885.

Keter Shem Tov. Zolkiew, 1794/95.

Kitvey Qodesh. Lvov, 1862.

Levi Yizhak of Berdichev. *Qedushat Levi ha-Shalem* (1811). Jerusalem, 1958.

Liqqutim Yeqarim. Lvov, 1792.

Maimonides, Moses. *Guide for the Perplexed*. Edited by Shelomo Pines. Chicago: University of Chicago Press, 1969.

Menahem of Recanati. *Ta'amey ha-Mizvot*. Constantinople, 1544.

Menahem Mendel of Vitebsk. *Peri ha-Arez*. Kapust, 1814.

Menahem Nahum of Chernobyl. *Me'or 'Eynayim*. Slavuta, 1798.

____. *Upright Practices* and *The Light of the Eyes*. New York: Paulist Press, 1982.

Moses Hayyim Ephraim of Sudilkov. *Degel Mahaneh Ephraim*. Korzec, 1811.

Nahman ben Simhah of Bratslav. *Liqqutey MoHaRaN*. Part one, Ostrog, 1808. Part two, Mohilev, 1811.

Poppers, Meir. *Liqqutey Torah . . . Ta'amey ha-Mizvot*. Vilna, 1880.

Ricci, Immanuel Hai. *Mishnat Hasidim*. Amsterdam, 1727.

Sa'adya ben Joseph, Gaon. *Book of Doctrines and Beliefs*. In *Three Jewish Philosophers*. Edited by Alexander Altmann. New York: Atheneum, 1969.

____. *Targum RaSaG la-Torah*. Edited by Moshe Zucker. New York: Jewish Theological Seminary, 1984.

Schneersohn, Menahem Mendel. *Derekh Mizvotekha*. Poltava, 1911–12.

Shemu'ah Tovah. Warsaw, 1938.

Shneur Zalman of Liadi. *Liqqutey Torah*. Zhitomir, 1848.

____. *Ma'amarim TaQSaB*. Brooklyn, 1964.

____. *Tanya* (*Liqqutey Amarim*). Slavuta, 1796–97.

____. *Torah Or*. Kapust, 1836.

Sternharz, Nathan. *Liqqutey Halakhot.* Jassy, 1843. Lvov, 1861.
Vital, Hayyim. [Attrib.] *Sefer ha-Kavvanot.* n.p., 1729[!]
___. *Sha'ar ha-Mizvot.* Jerusalem, 1905.
Zava'at RYVaSH. Zolkiew, n.d. [179-?]
Zemah, Jacob. *Nagid u-Mezavveh.* Jerusalem, 1965.
Ze'ev Wolf of Zhitomir. *Or ha-Me'ir.* Korzec, 1798.
Zvi Elimelech of Dinov. *Derekh Pequdekha.* Lvov, 1851.

II. Modern Authors

Baer, Yitzhak. *A History of the Jews in Christian Spain.* Vol. 1.
    Philadelphia: Jewish Publication Society, 1978.
Bamberger, Bernard. "Revelations of Torah After Sinai," *HUCA*
    16 (1941): 97–113.
Ben-Shelomo, Yosef. *Torat ha-Elohut shel Rabbi Moshe Cordovero.*
    Jerusalem: Mossad Bialik, 1965.
Biale, David. *Gershom Scholem: Kabbalah and Counter-History.* 2nd
    ed. Cambridge, Mass.: Harvard University Press, 1987.
Bialik, Hayyim Nahman. "Revealment and Concealment in
    Language," translated in *Modern Hebrew Literature*, edited by
    Robert Alter. New York: Behrman House, 1975, pp. 109–24.
Buber, Martin. "Interpreting Hasidism." *Commentary* 36 (1963):
    218–25.
___. "The Life of the Hasidim." Book 3 in *Hasidism and Modern
    Man.* New York: Harper and Row, 1966.
___. "Symbolic and Sacramental Existence." Chapter 5 in
    The Origin and Meaning of Hasidism. New York: Harper and
    Row, 1960.
Davies, William David. *Torah in the Messianic Age and/or the Age
    to Come.* Philadelphia: Society of Biblical Literature, 1952.
Dubnov, Simeon. *Toledot Ha-Hasidut.* Tel Aviv: Dvir, 1960.
Elior, Rachel. "HaBaD, the Contemplative Ascent to God,"
    In *Jewish Spirituality II.* New York: Crossroad, 1987, pp.
    157–205.
___. *The Theory of Divinity of Hasidut HaBaD.* Jerusalem: Magnes
    Press, 1982 (Hebrew); New York: SUNY Press, 1993 (English).
Fine, Lawrence. "The Contemplative Practice of Yihudim in

Lurianic Kabbalah," in *Jewish Spirituality II*. New York: Crossroad, 1987, pp. 64–98.

Ginzberg, Louis. *The Legends of the Jews*. Philadelphia: Jewish Publication Society, 1968.

Goodenough, Erwin, R. *By Light, Light*. New Haven: Yale University Press, 1935.

___. "Paul and the Hellenization of Christianity," in *Religions in Antiquity*, edited by Jacob Neusner. Leiden: E. J. Brill, 1968.

Green, Arthur. "Hasidism: Discovery and Retreat," in *The Other Side of God*, edited by Peter Berger. Garden City, N. Y.: Anchor Press, 1981, pp. 104–30.

___. "On Translating Hasidic Homilies," *Prooftexts* 3: 1 (1983): 63–72.

___. "Teachings of the Hasidic Masters," in *Back to the Sources*, edited by Barry W. Holtz. New York: Schocken, 1984, pp. 361–401.

___. *Tormented Master: A Life of Rabbi Nahman of Bratslav*. Tuscaloosa: University of Alabama Press, 1979.

___. "Typologies of Leadership and the Hasidic Zaddiq," in *Jewish Spirituality II*. New York: Crossroad, 1987, pp. 127–56.

Heinemann, Isaac. *Ta'amey ha-Mizvot be-Sifrut Yisra'el*. Jerusalem: World Zionist Organization, 1959.

Heschel, Abraham J. *The Circle of the Baal Shem Tov*. Chicago: University of Chicago Press, 1985.

___. *Torah Min ha-Shamayim*. 2 vols. London: Soncino Press, 1962–65.

Horodezky, Shmuel Abba. *Ha-Mistorin be-Yisra'el*. Tel Aviv: Aggudat ha-Sofrim, 1961.

Jacobs, Louis. *Seeker of Unity*. New York: Basic Books, 1966.

___. "The Uplifting of Sparks in Later Jewish Mysticism," in *Jewish Spirituality II*. New York: Crossroad, 1987, pp. 99–126.

Joel, Manuel. *Blicke in die Religionsgeschichte*. Breslau: Verlag Schottlaender, 1880–83.

Katz, Jacob. *Tradition and Crisis*. New York: Schocken, 1971.

Koenig, Natan Zvi. *Neveh Zaddiqim*. Beney Beraq, 1969.

Lieberman, Chaim. *Ohel Rachel*. 3 vols. New York, 1980–84.

Lieberman, Saul. *Tosefta ki-Feshutah*. New York: Jewish Theological

Seminary of America, 1955.

Loewenthal, H. J. T. C. "The Concept of Mesirat Nefesh ('Self-Sacrifice') in the Teachings of R. Dov Baer of Lubavitch." Ph.D. dissertation, University of London, 1981.

Mahler, Raphael. *Hasidism and Haskalah*. Philadelphia: Jewish Publication Society, 1985.

Margulies, Reuven. *Sha'arey Zohar*. Jerusalem: Mossad Harav Kook, 1956.

Marmorstein, Arthur. *The Doctrine of Merits in Old Rabbinic Literature*. Vol. 2. New York: Ktav, 1968.

Matt, Daniel. "The Mystic and the Mizvot," in *Jewish Spirituality I*. New York: Crossroad, 1986, pp. 367–404.

Mendes-Flohr, Paul. "Law and Sacrament: Ritual Observance in Twentieth-Century Jewish Thought," in *Jewish Spirituality II*. New York: Crossroad, 1987, pp. 321–22.

Newman, Eugene. *Life and Teachings of Isaiah Horowitz*. London: E. Newman, 1972.

Nietzsche, Friedrich Wilhelm. *The Birth of Tragedy* (1872). New York: Gordon Press, 1974.

Preuss, Julius. *Biblisch-Talmudische Medizin*. Berlin: S. Karger, 1923.

Rosenberg, Joel. "Biblical Tradition: Literature and Spirit in Ancient Israel," in *Jewish Spirituality I*. New York: Crossroad, 1986, pp. 82–89.

Sanders, E. P. *Paul and Palestinian Judaism*. Philadelphia: Fortress Press, 1977.

Sandmel, Samuel. *The Genius of Paul*. Philadelphia: Fortress Press, 1979.

____. *Paul and Rabbinic Judaism*. Philadelphia: Fortress Press, 1980.

____. "Philo's Place in Judaism," Part II. *HUCA* 26 (1955): 151–332.

Schatz-Uffenheimer, Rivka. "Anti-spiritualism ba-hasidut," *Molad* 171 (1962): 513–28.

____. *Ha-Hasidut ke-Mystiqah*. Jerusalem: Magnes Press, 1968.

Schneersohn, Joseph Isaac. *The Tsemah Tsedek and the Haskalah Movement*. Brooklyn, N.Y.: Kehot, 1946.

Scholem, Gershom. "Ha-Im Hibber Rabbi Moshe de Leon et Sefer ha-Shem?" *Kiryat Sefer* 1 (1924): 45–52.

____. "Hitpathut Torat ha-'Olamot be-Qabbalat ha-Rishonim." *Tarbiz* 2 (1931): 415ff and *Tarbiz* 3 (1932): 33ff.

____. *Major Trends in Jewish Mysticism*. New York: Schocken, 1941.

____. "Martin Buber's Interpretation of Hasidism" in *The Messianic Idea in Judaism and Other Essays*. New York: Schocken, 1971, pp. 228–50.

____. "The Meaning of Torah in Jewish Mysticism" in *On the Kabbalah and Its Symbolism*. New York: Schocken, 1965.

____. *Origins of the Kabbalah*. Philadelphia: Jewish Publication Society, 1987.

____. "Redemption Through Sin" in *The Messianic Idea in Judaism and Other Essays*. New York: Schocken, 1971, pp. 78–141.

____. *Sabbatai Sevi*. Princeton: Princeton University Press, 1973.

Septimus, Bernard. *Hispano-Jewish Culture in Transition*. Cambridge: Harvard University Press, 1982.

Stanislawski, Michael. *Tsar Nicholas I and the Jews*. Philadelphia: Jewish Publication Society, 1983.

Strack, Hermann, and Billerbeck, Adolf. *Kommentar zum neuen Testament aus Talmud und Midrasch*. 4 Aufl. München: Beck, 1965–69.

Talmage, Frank. "Apples of Gold," in *Jewish Spirituality I*. New York: Crossroad, 1986, pp. 313–55.

Urbach, Ephraim E. "Halacha and Prophecy," *Tarbiz* 18 (1947): 1–27.

____. *The Sages*. Jerusalem: Magnes Press, 1975.

____. "When Old Prophecy Ceased," *Tarbiz* 17 (1946): 1–11.

Von Rad, Gerhard. *Genesis: A Commentary*. Philadelphia: Westminster Press, 1972, pp. 270–71.

Von Seters, John. *Abraham in History and Tradition*. New Haven: Yale University Press, 1975.

Weinryb, Bernard. *The Jews of Poland*. Philadelphia: Jewish Publication Society, 1972.

Weiss, Joseph G. *Mehqarim be-Hasidut Braslav*. Jerusalem: Mossad Bialik, 1974.

____. *Studies in Eastern European Jewish Mysticism*. Oxford: Oxford University Press, 1985.

____. "Talmud Torah le-Shittat Rabbi Yisra'el BeSHT," in *Israel*

Brodie Festschrift. London: Jews' College, 1966, Hebrew section, pp. 151–69.

Westermann, Claus. *Genesis 12–36: A Commentary.* Minneapolis: Augsburg Publishing House, 1985.

Wilensky, Mordecai. *Ḥasidim u-Mitnaggedim.* 2 vols. Jerusalem: Mossad Bialik, 1970.